MW01242190

AN
OKLAHOMA
ORIGINAL

The Life and Career of
Paul E. "Pete" Simmons

AN
OKLAHOMA
ORIGINAL

by
Jan Collins

A BOLD TRUTH Publication
Christian Literature & Artwork

In memory of

Howard C. Fisher
Patti Reeves Wilson
Norma Jean Wilson
Barbara Waggoner Harper
E.D. Loyd
James T. "Jimmy" Stevenson

AN OKLAHOMA ORIGINAL
Copyright © 2015 Jan Collins

ISBN 13: 978-0-9904376-9-7

BOLD TRUTH PUBLISHING
300 West 41st Street
Sand Springs, Oklahoma 74063
www.BoldTruthPublishing.com
beirep@yahoo.com

Printed in the USA. All rights reserved under International Copyright Law. All contents and/or cover art and design may not be reproduced in whole or in part in any form without the express written consent of the Author.

DEDICATION

To My Husband, Kenny Collins
Who has loved and supported me
Unconditionally for 42 years

To My Daughters,
Laura Hopkins and Mollie Moses
Who knew and loved their Daddy Pete
I wanted them to see him through my eyes

To My Sons-in-Law,
Jonathan Hopkins and Blake Moses
I love you like sons, I am blessed to
Have you in our family

To My Grandchildren and Future
Grandchildren and Great-Grandchildren
Audrey Grace Hopkins
Troy Lee, Clay Thomas and Judd Ryan Moses

In memory of Mother and Daddy
I love and miss you but know
We will meet again

To the Many Descendants of
Stephen B. and Mollie C. Simmons

CONTENTS

FOREWORD

It is doubtful that anyone could provide biographical information of the late Paul Emmett Simmons with such a personal touch as well as that penned by his daughter, Jan Simmons Collins.

When Jan told me that she was going to write a book about the life of her Dad, whom most of us knew as "Pete," I wondered to myself, "How in the world can she really capture the essence—the heart, soul and spirit—of such a unique, complex man?" I was hopeful for her but must admit was also a bit skeptical. That skepticism changed quickly as I listened to her talk with enthusiasm about some of the stories she wanted to share about her Father.

Who could recall those real life stories better than Jan, the oldest daughter in the family? No one. She is part of the story. Those memories are recorded in a very nostalgic way. Her goal to complete the book during the year of the 100th anniversary of her father's birth makes the book even more special.

Father-daughter relationships are unique, with each having particular esteem and affection for the other. Recent studies conducted by university researchers in England and the United States show that fathers provide unique benefits to their daughter through their active and positive presence from the time of birth throughout adulthood. Such a relationship is reflected in the stories you are about to read and enjoy. You will find, as an ancient King once wrote in the book of Ecclesiastes about the mystery of time, "There is an occasion for everything . . . a time to weep and a time to laugh." Both emotions will be felt as you read the pages that follow.

Most of us who knew Paul "Pete" Simmons remember the man from his public life. There was much more to his life. This is a man whose deeply religious beliefs at one time seemed to be leading him to be a preacher. He would have been a contemporary of Evangelist Oral Roberts. Instead, he became a lawyer. The reflection on the "what if" question reveals a part of Pete's life than many, even close friends, did not know. Jan shares the more intimate side of him as her "Dad." Only she can tell the story from that perspective.

In addition to writing about those very personal stories, Jan Collins has sprinkled into the chapters some brief tales told by friends who relate their own experiences with this unusual man. Those observations contribute to helping understand this very complex man.

Reading these personal stories about the Simmons family is a bit like sitting in an audience at a play, not unlike Thornton Wilder's classic Our Town, Most of us have watched and listened, admittedly a bit teary-eyed, during some stage production of Our Town. A special scene in the play is when the key character, Emily Webb, after her death, returns home as apparition—reflecting on one day, her 12th birthday. She witnesses the mundane, ordinary, everyday doings, connections, and family activities of that single day.

At one point, frustrated by her invisibility, she pleads: "Oh, Mama, just look at me one minute as though you really saw me!" She was 12 and is trying to speak now to her mother, but of course her mother can only say the things she said to her when she was 12, and can't respond. Emily finally just stops and says, "It goes so fast. Life, it just goes by so fast, and we don't have time to look at each other."

Well, she was right.

Life goes by so quickly! Our daily lives, filled with home and family activities and demanding work responsibilities can become so busy and chaotic that we don't have time to look at each other, to stop and really appreciate each other. That is unfortunate.

The stories about the life of every person should be remembered and shared in some manner—passed on to children, grandchildren and great-grandchildren so that each of us in descendent generation will better understand our heritage. Jan Simmons Collins has done so in the pages of this wonderful book of reflections on some of the incidents in the life of Pete Simmons and how he impacted the lives of so many of us who were privileged to know this unusual man—truly an Oklahoma Original!

Clarence G. Oliver, Jr., Ed.D.
Educator, Journalist, Historian and
Author of —
One from the Least and Disappearing Generation.
Tony Dufflebag . . . and Other Remembrances
        of the War in Korea,
A Time of Peace, Season of Innocence

ACKNOWLEDGMENTS

Until the writing of this book, I did not know how many people could be involved in seeing it to fruition. First of all I want to acknowledge that God dropped this desire into my heart. It was confirmed when I visited with Dr. Clarence G. Oliver, Jr. at a patriotic program at Broken Arrow's newest middle school a few years ago. He was one of many people who continually told me a story about my dad. Without Dr. Oliver's encouragement, patience and expertise, I may not have persevered. With his demanding schedule of serving on boards, committees and constant community work, I do not take lightly how valuable Dr. Oliver's time is. Words alone can not really express how much I appreciate all he has done to teach and assist me in this experience, not to mention the hours he devoted to editing this book. Although Dr. Oliver is many years younger than my dad, he has been like a surrogate father during this project partly because of their similar literary mindsets.

To Mike Singer, whose story is probably the dearest and most important story to me personally. I am forever grateful to him for stopping me in a restaurant in 1999 to tell me the story that provided the substance for my book.

I also could not have finished this project in this amount of time had it not been for my husband, Kenny to allow me to unplug from life for awhile, putting many things on "hold" while I pressed on to publish this within the same year of what would have been the 100th birthday of my dad's birth. Kenny understands more than anyone else how important this book is for me to complete. I acknowledge and appreciate as well, my daughters, Laura and Mollie, their husbands and children for allowing me to work on my project during a few family times. They have all been encouraging.

To my brother and sister, Chris and Barbara Simmons who lived much of this book with me, but may remember events differently through the years.

To my high school friend Kathy Friend Brumley, who was the first to read my chapter headings while Kenny and I were in Pensacola in for a Navy squadron reunion in September and simply said, "I know of a publisher in your area."

To Aaron Jones, of Bold Truth Publishing Company, who took this project by faith. He has proved to be a true blessing, not only because of his talent as a graphic designer, but as a compassionate man of integrity. He exhibited great patience as we carefully placed the pictures I chose for this book.

I acknowledge friends like Jim King, Hoil and Mahala Thompson, J.D. and Norma Wilson and Barbara Harper who attended a reception that the family held to commemorate what would have been Daddy's 100th birthday. Jim King was a pro-tégé and colleague of my dad's from the early years. Barbara Harper was one of our first neighbors and shared good memo-ries with us that day. Hoil and Mahala and the Wesley Sunday School class from the early 1950's were all long-time residents of Broken Arrow and life-time friends of Mother and Daddy.

I acknowledge friends like Mary Kay Baird, Jill Edwards Steeley and Dianna Heginbotham who share a love for reading and as a labor of love, they read and reread my manuscript and were honest with me about the flow of the book. I reminded Mary Kay this is not a thesis, but just memoirs and stories for family history; she reminded me of the importance to have in-tegrity of correctness. Although she is not a native of this area and did not know many of our hometown people, she was able to follow the genealogy and very honestly had to tell me when she could not. Mary Kay has several authors in her own family and guided me with her knowledge and expertise. I am most appreciative that she kept me on target even when it meant I had to rewrite paragraphs, stories and even chapters.

Jill brought with her over forty-three years of teaching and writing experience. She has a sharp eye for detail. I am so glad she managed to juggle time in between teaching classes at ORU to assist me.

When asked to read the manuscript for content and flow, I appreciated Dianna's willingness to join us with her honesty having already heard some of the stories.

To Debbie Linzy Overstreet, Robert J. Stubblefield and Judge Dennis N. Shook whose professions were developed and influenced by my dad. For Debbie, my dad's bailiff and legal secretary and who probably knew him best besides our family members and in many ways knew him more. She felt like a daughter to him. Debbie and I have had recent opportunities to reminisce about many of my special times shared with Daddy in his latter years. For Robert, who seemed to be a second son to Pete and Judge Shook both as ardent observers who learned from an expert in their field, and achieved great accomplishments of their own. He would be proud of all three.

To Sharon Champlin, fellow researcher and active member of DAR Creek Lands Chapter of Broken Arrow, Oklahoma; Lori Lewis, Director of the Broken Arrow Historical Museum and Michelle Hadley who patiently supplied my requests for finding pictures. I would not have been able to achieve the detailed history within this book without their assistance in researching information and pictures.

To all of my Simmons, Peterson and Neighbors cousins who unknowingly provided family history and information through the years in what we probably never guessed would be in this form of print. I acknowledge that my mother, Frances Jenni Simmons and my Great Aunt Eva Faye Neighbors Newcomb began the genealogical research over fifty years ago with accurate documentation. To LaVerne Collins Fry, Dorothy Collins

Bowers, James Paul Collins, Sandy Collins Walker, John Edward Collins and Linda Collins Dimon, whose invaluable contributions as well as the many hours of fun and fond memories provided while visiting Grandma Mollie Burns and Aunt Kathryn Collins in Kansas City, Missouri. Without Linda and Sandy's love for research, Mother and Aunt Faye's work may not have been continued.

To my Broken Arrow cousins Jo Ann Simmons Smith who I knew the best, I appreciate the stories and contributions she gave about Grandpa Simmons and World War II information about her dad, Uncle James and tying it all together toward the end. To her brothers Steve and Jimmy who were part of our history. To Jerry and Paul Simmons and Marian Simmons Dick, whose dad lived longer than any of the other siblings I acknowledge and appreciate hand-written note-taking, visits and their participation at our family reunions through the years. As Uncle Earl's and Uncle Jim's children, they provided memories from our Thanksgiving and other holidays together at Uncle Jim's egg farm.

To John Edgar Newcomb, Aunt Faye's oldest son and present at our first family reunion for love of family history, for his tedious documentation through the years to preserve what his mother collected and wrote and for his wonderful Grandpa Neighbors' cowboy stories. To Nancy Lynne Newcomb-Davis, John's daughter, who I have only met recently. I appreciate your exuberance and love for family history. To Priscilla Newcomb Schneider, John's younger sister and who holds the prestigious spot as the "youngest" grandchild of John Henry and Ida Lee Neighbors who provided information about the loving and fun side to Ida Lee. To Cindy Green Sanders for allowing me to use her mother Coralee German Green's information as we reconnected to our roots.

To Mary Riseling Woodward and Betty Riseling Kellams, my dear Peterson cousins who I had the opportunity of meeting years ago. I acknowledge the invaluable family history that you have provided along with introducing me to your brother Lawrence "Bo" Riseling, Jr. To Bob and Margie Peterson who I have enjoyed seeing through the years on Broken Arrow Pioneer Day and class reunions. Thank you for the information you provided on Bob's grandfather Charles who traveled from Sweden with a story of his own. To Betty Peterson Stevenson and her husband Jimmy, who I have been connected with for many years through my mother.

For the many people who my dad has helped legally or have been touched by his compassion in other ways, from friends at the First Methodist Church to his secretaries and law associates. To his first high school secretaries the Sherrell sisters: Shirley Sherrell Kates, Susanne "Sudie" Sherrell Cypert and Peggy Sherrell VanDyke I acknowledge your stories of appreciation to my dad. To Mary Ruth Roberts Megee, one of his first fulltime secretaries, to Yvonne Morgan who joined his office later on South Main both of whom provided information, funny stories and dates to assist with proper timelines, I am appreciative.

To the countless Broken Arrow High School graduates from early 1950's through many decades later, who have started conversations with me at Pioneer Dinners or class reunions and mixers like, "I have a story to tell you about your dad." I have tried to do your stories justice. To the many businessmen and people like Dr. James R. Newcomb who knew my dad on Main Street of Broken Arrow and had stories that I hope I was able to fit into the book, I gratefully acknowledge.

Interviews

Wanda Foster
Tammy Posey
Mrs. Frankie Posey
Van Kunze
Mike Lester
Jack Ross, Jr.
Bill Autry
Berniece Castleberry
Mrs. Mildred Ree
Larry Pennington
John "J.W." Scott
Nick Hood, Jr.

Janice Mallow Hood
Lynn Bertling
Carol Bertling
Sue Ann Scace
E.D. Loyd
Frances Dill Loyd
Dennie Crawford
Charlie Gann
Howard Fisher
Arlis Wilson
Ronnie Penny
Linda Johnson Penny

Karen Jennings Treat
Butch Mays
Amy Morris Marcoux
Marcella Burgess Giles
Connie Tucker Collins
Gladys Tucker Coshow
Gary Smith
O.T. "Andy" Anderson
Clyde Cline
Johnnie Parks
Johnnie Lofton
Barbara Samuel
Leland Grubb

INTRODUCTION

Paul E. "Pete" Simmons was first dubbed 'An Oklahoma Original' by a television reporter from Tulsa, Oklahoma. He was definitely a one-of-a-kind individual. Pete was as versatile in his personality as he was in his God-given gifts and talents. He evolved from a Master Sergeant in the Marine Corps on Guadalcanal during World War II to a Sunday school teacher for over 35 years. Some called him eccentric when riding his CB750A Hondamatic motorcycle to court when serving as Associate District Judge. Others called him friend and close confidant, and believed he was one of the best judges and defense attorneys in northeastern Oklahoma.

As a daughter of a lawyer, municipal judge, community leader, city councilman, mayor, and later an associate district judge, it may have appeared I had special privileges. In fact at times I felt ostracized by certain families who were my age because of my dad's boldness. Anyone who lived in the Broken Arrow area during the 50's, 60's, 70's and 80's knew how outspoken and unfiltered my dad could be.

I believed Daddy was a good lawyer and helped a lot of people through the years. My impression was more people were opposed to his views than for them. I also had the opinion he was too strict. Now I know he kept me on the straight and narrow. I carried that perception of his sternness through our relationship for years.

When I began attending Pioneer Dinners and interacting with people with whom I had grown up, remembering them from church, or as secretaries for daddy, or just town and business people, often I would have to introduce myself to them. By way of letting them know my family connection, it would be necessary to say, "I'm Paul and Frances Simmons' daughter......Pete Simmons," pausing and looking for a negative reaction. Usually a huge grin would appear across their faces as they would recall a favorite story about him or let me know he was the "best lawyer around.   " Mildred Ree, "old" Dr. Onis Franklin's nurse was one of those people. Now as an adult instead of just Pete's daughter, my perception of Daddy is different. This book is about my perception of Paul E. "Pete" Simmons.

In Daddy's latter years we often discussed the word "perception" and what this word meant. Philosophical discussions were something Daddy thoroughly enjoyed. Debate would be a closer fit to describing it. I was generally no match for him because of his strong opinions. He was not easily swayed. As two adults, our respect for each other's philosophies changed. Looking back, those were special times.

This book began as a tiny seed planted in my heart when Mike Singer shared an unusual story about Daddy. Then a few years later another incident happened. I was at a patriotic event in 2003 at Broken Arrow's newest middle school. After the program I was browsing through a display of pictures of the school district when Dr. Clarence G. Oliver, Jr. a former Broken Arrow Public School Superintendent approached me. He told me a familiar story except he added new details I had not heard. My interest was certainly piqued by the historical information he shared that day. It proved to be much more than just an enjoyable story.

From the encounter with Dr. Oliver, I contemplated the stories told about Daddy. There must be other stories about Daddy's early years in Broken Arrow. These historical stories about Pete Simmons should be shared from the people of Broken Arrow and surrounding communities.

This journey began as a book of memoirs for our family so it contains lots of family names and information. For the genealogist, I have included detail to follow the trail. For the lover of history and stories about adventure, I attempted to eliminate unnecessary or irrelevant information for easier reading. I enjoyed putting my dad's stories in print and hope the reader does as well.

I concluded that some people only knew him from a distance or from the outside, but those who knew him well understood, respected and loved him. This book depicts his good times and bad; his turmoil and triumphs. But it mostly shows a tender-hearted unique man underneath the tough image. You will be able to relate to the humanness of Pete, his life and career.

Jan Collins

May 5, 2015

Paul E. Simmons, 6 months old, Rock Hill, Oklahoma

Chapter 1
BORN IN A LOG CABIN

Only seven years after statehood, Paul Emmett Simmons was born in Oilton, Oklahoma, on Friday, November 13, 1914. He often humorously boasted that both Abraham Lincoln and he were born in log cabins. The year 2014 marked the 100th year of his birth. This particular year seemed to be fitting to tell my dad's story.

In 1988 Daddy wanted to try to find "his" log cabin. I drove him to Oilton to see if any remains of the cabin were still standing. Daddy drew a rough map from his recollection of where the cabin was located. According to his map, it was not too far from Buckeye School. Unfortunately, the school was no longer there nor was the log cabin.

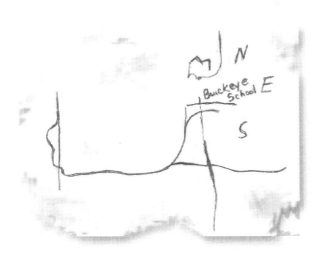

Pete drew this recollection of "his" log cabin in Oilton, Oklahoma.

Oilton Quest Renewed

I recently visited the Oilton area to get a sense of the geography in an attempt to visualize how the area appeared in that era before highways were built. Daddy was born in a time of log and sod houses and the roadways were traveled by wagons and buggies. Because our dad instilled a love for geography, history and travel into all three of his children, I was curious as to how these pioneer families came to Oklahoma and how they came to know each other. It was always interesting to me "why" Paul Emmett Simmons' parents told him about this birthplace.

My desire to write factual and historical information about Paul Emmett and his beginnings in Oilton was more important than penning the excitement of rumors and legends. Therefore, even as this book was well on its way to completion, I felt an urgency to go to the area that he described, to see how accurate he was. After only one phone call, I immediately was in touch with people who remembered Buckeye School, who were aware of its location and most importantly actually knew information about this legendary "log cabin."

My first contact in Oilton was Wanda Foster, a busy lady who is not only in local government as a member of the city council, but also a member of the Oilton Chamber of Commerce. I found she was very knowledgeable about Oilton and a lady who loved to talk about its history. She was definitely a great find for my first phone call in this quest.

During this research, I was told that Oilton did not become a town officially until 1915. Wanda explained that the log cabin near Buckeye school which my dad talked about was located in an area known as Silver City. At the mere mention of a log cabin close to Buckeye School, Wanda filled in the blanks and connected the dots of the significance of this particular log cabin.

Oklahoma Cowboys

It is believed that the land in the Silver City area and beyond was once an Indian allotment assigned to certain members of the Muscogee Creek tribe. Because many Creek Indians sided with the Confederacy during the Civil War, they had to forfeit their treaty rights according to the United States and had a possibility of having their property confiscated. After the Civil War, many Indians in the Oilton area began allowing the white man to lease land for cattle raising and farming. Unfortunately many white men began marrying Indian women not only to avoid paying rent but moreover to obtain tribal membership. Once allowed into this cattle-grazing land, their numbers increased.

A Texas cattleman, by the name of Blair, arrived after the Civil War. Blair secured large tracts of ranch land in the Oilton area from the Indian Department. Estimated to have covered more than 100,000 acres of what is now Oilton, Blair ranch extended to the north with the Cimarron River as a boundary, to the east then south of Mannford about five miles, then two miles east and south of Olive.

Wallace Doolin was hired as foreman of Blair's ranch in 1884. Blair Ranch was later owned by Wallace Doolin by 1921. Wallace Doolin and M.P. Tippin both owned ranches in Oilton. Many of Doolin's descendants still live in the vicinity of Oilton. History indicated that this area was populated by cowboys. Anytime cowboys were living in an area, rodeos would eventually follow. Doolin Ranch advertised a rodeo in 1921.

The largest number on record for Blair Ranch of cattle fed through the season was estimated to be 17,800. The first headquarters used by Blair was a double log house probably large enough to accommodate a passel of cowboys during a dinner meal. Double log indicated it was actually a two-story log house,

"THE ROUND UP"
DOOLIN'S RANCH, OILTON, OKLAHOMA
Sunday, August 21, 1921

Roping Contest—First and Second Day's Time

Broncho Riding Contest

Bull Dogging Contest

Diablo Banter's Busters—Ten Dollars a minute for any one to ride
this mule. Positively not "white"

WILD COW MILKING

RELAY RACE

STEER RIDING---Purse $10.00; $5.00 and $2.50

WILD HORSE RACE—Purse Fifteen, Ten and Five Dollars

DOOLIN & SONS, Managers

LOUNSBURY, Secretary.   HENRY GRAMMER, Arena Director.
SHIRE, Treasurer.   DOC C. W. PARDEE, Announcer.

"The Round-Up" Doolin Ranch, Oilton, Oklahoma,
Friday, August 19, 1921"
• Courtesy of Drumright Historical Society - Drumright, Oklahoma

located about 500 to 600 feet west of Hamp Daily's corner in the
Silver City area and later housed the cowboys who ran the cattle
across this vast land. If it were indeed a log cabin then perhaps
it was the one in which Paul Emmett was born. This double log
house was later used as a school until Buckeye School could be

built. Daddy often spoke of the Simmons and Doolin families as friends. Silver City and Oilton definitely were thriving environments for cowboys during that time.

In the spring of 1911, Blair went to Osage County, Oklahoma, and gave up his leases in the Oilton area. That was about the time one young man living in that area may have worked cattle, had just turned 25 years of age and perhaps had thoughts of settling down. That young man would have been Stephen Boles Simmons, Paul Emmett Simmons' father.

Special effort has been made to establish the places where the Simmons families and their relatives settled in Oilton then in the Broken Arrow, Oklahoma area. My mission is to track Paul Emmett Simmons' beginnings, detailing enough family history for genealogists to track yet easy enough to follow without becoming too labor intensive. Perhaps, as my Dad would have done, I have attempted to sprinkle in bits of the beginnings of Oklahoma's history as well.

Oklahoma Outlaws

Inhabitants of the early years of Oklahoma were Indians, pioneers and outlaws. The southeastern United States was the ancestral land of The Five Civilized Tribes: Cherokee, Choctaw, Chickasaw, Creek and Seminole. They were removed to what was called Indian Territory after the Civil War. These Five Tribes had well-developed legal and law enforcement systems, but no jurisdiction over the white man. The only court in Indian Territory to govern white man was the Federal District Court for the Western District of Arkansas. Most people in Oklahoma either know of this single judge who resided over this district court, whether by history books or from the movie theatres.

Judge Isaac Parker sat on the bench from 1875 until 1896.

Although he was nicknamed "The Hangin' Judge," he was known to be fair and impartial. He was a God-fearing devout man and devoted to his family. It has been said he often urged the defendants who were sentenced to hang to make peace with their creator as he preached a persuasive message to them from the bench.

With the first Oklahoma Land Run of 1889 and other runs following, many white settlers came here hoping to become land owners in search of better lives and to raise families. During these times, Oklahoma was also known to be a haven for outlaws, some hardened and feared by many. Many sought hiding places and shelters in the various caves and caverns throughout the state, particularly in the southeastern part of Indian Territory, west of Ft. Smith, Arkansas. One such cavern is now known as Robbers' Cave is located in a State Park which bears that name. One's imagination can conjure up names of famous outlaws who may have hidden in one of these caverns such as the Dalton gang, the Doolin gang, Belle Starr, Jesse James, Arkansas Tom and Bitter Creek Newcomb.

In 1893, these latter two were in the famous Battle of Ingalls in which Bill Doolin lost his life. Located in Payne County only 10 miles east of Stillwater, Ingalls was one of the most thriving trading and agricultural sections of Oklahoma Territory. Some of Ingalls' citizens who may have been present during that famous shoot out coincidentally have some of the same last names of people who are related to the Simmons family. Although no definite connections were ever made to our Simmons family, some of the citizens interested in furthering the well-being of their community were John South, J.A. Simmons, Joseph Simmons, and Robert VanArsdale, whose names provided interesting fuel for the fire.

Family Involvement

My Mother, Frances Jenni Simmons, took an interest in re-searching family history from the early 1970's. By the mid-eight-ies, Mother had accumulated quite a collection of genealogy that could be compared to the work of any professional genealogist. Recorded by hand and on a manual typewriter, she diligently doc-umented information that she collected in addition to what oth-ers had shared with her. She corresponded with several people, whether related to our family or not, constantly in search of those who could be linked to our lineage. Some of her favorite penpals from Ft. Smith, Arkansas, were descendants of Belle Starr.

Not having been an active researcher until that time, Paul Emmett became interested in the genealogy search, perhaps for the sake of finding "infamous" relatives. Maybe being related to outlaws was more exciting to him as to be related to a famous president or inventor. For several years, there was talk about possibly being related to the Doolin or Dalton gangs. So the research continued. There was even discussion of Paul Emmett Simmons being named after Emmett Doolin or Emmett Dal-ton. I continued to inquire and dig for the truth.

The Simmons Family Makes Their Way to Oklahoma

Research and curiosity began with the discovery of James and Anna Whittington Simmons. Coming from Kentucky, this family perhaps had up to eleven children— nine sons and two daughters. Several members of the Simmons family have been difficult to trace at times and often found in different states. James and Anna's children were born in Illinois, Indiana, Mis-souri, and Kansas. There has been strong evidence pointing to the fact many of the Simmons families moved often and were not on census reports, but it was not always clear as to whether drifting or moving in search of work. The Simmons family had good horsemanship abilities, probably due to at least five of the nine Simmons sons being soldiers in the Civil War. There was speculation some rode with outlaw gangs, were friends of those outlaws or were just plain ol' cowboys.

There were several Simmons sons on the 1864 Kansas Militia Muster Rolls from the Civil War along with some others related to them. The soldiers who were James and Anna's sons were B.W. (Benjamin Whittington) Simmons, James Simmons, Joseph Simmons, J.W. (John Wesley Simmons). These particular sons came to Arkansas and Oklahoma. The South and Sutton brothers on this roll later became relatives by marriage.

Rebecca Jane and Nancy Ellen with their father, James Simmons

Although James Simmons was born in Indiana, he met and married Mercy Elizabeth Sutton in Kansas. They held a double wedding with James' brother, John Wesley Simmons and Emily Jane Jackson in 1862. Ironically, a census showed that both couples had sons named James born in 1863, one of whom came to Muskogee but later settled in Broken Arrow.

James and Mercy's youngest daughters Rebecca Jane and Nancy Ellen were born in Muskogee, Indian Territory, in 1879 and 1881 respectively. Many people from Broken Arrow remember them as Jane Moore and Ellen Peterson Cannon.

In 1880, there was a letter written to The Honorable Samuel

Checote, Principal Chief by members of the Muscogee Creek Nation on James Simmons' behalf because he was "non-citizen". He apparently had a mule of good stock and the tribe was requesting he be allowed to stay in their Nation in order to offer his mule for services.

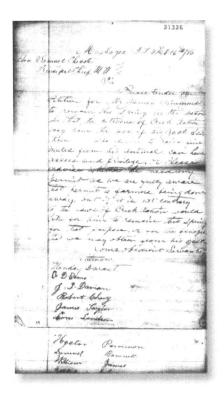

*Letter to Honorable
Samuel Checote, Principal Chief of
Muscogee Creek Tribe*

---

*31326
Muskogee I.T. February 16th, 1880
Monday, Durant*

*Hon. Samuel Checote
Principal Chief, M.N.
Please tender our Petition for Mr. James Simmons
to remain this spring in the nation so that the citizens*

13

of Creek Nation may have the use of his jack ass. Those who desire to raise fine mules from his animal can have access and privilege.

Or please advise whether he need any permit as we are fully aware that permits to farmers being done away, but if it is not contrary to the laws of Creek Nation would like for him to remain this spring for that purpose of for the benefit that we may obtain from his jack ass.

Your obedient Servants,
Petitioners

A.D. Bemo	*J.T. Davison*
Robert Cheny	*James Taylor*
Cass Lamkin	*Hector Persimmon*
Samuel Baronett	*William James*
Jessie Johnson	*Bustin Hawkins*
William Landress	*William Carves*
John D. Bimmer	*James Cobb*
C. H. Davis	*Sage Burwell*
John H. Henderson	*Davis Dickson*
James Curnal	*Nettie Gland*
Adam McIntosh	*Jimmie McIntosh*
John A. Myers	*Mack Cobb*
Deac Simpson	*Samuel Johnson*

James and Mercy apparently migrated northwest of Muskogee within the next few years because their youngest son, Stephen Boles was born in Tulsa, Indian Territory, in 1885. Stephen was the father of Paul Emmett Simmons. By 1900 James, Mercy and Stephen moved further west into Creek County.

The Family Connection in Oilton

James and Mercy Simmons   *John Wesley and Clara Biddle Simmons with grandchildren*

As many families did in those pioneer days, they may have been related to some of the families who lived close by or even next door. Such is true with the Simmons' in Oklahoma. Some of the families who were also in and around Oilton and Jennings during this time were Petersons, Thompsons, Creeks, and Neighbors. Those family names were in that area and on the 1900 Federal Census records, living in Township 19 of Creek County, Oklahoma. They were James and Mercy Simmons, along with his brother John Wesley. John Wesley was listed with his second wife, Clara Biddle. His first wife Emily Jane Jackson Simmons died in 1888. Also living at Oilton at the time were some Petersons and Neighbors families. All four of these families are related to Paul Emmett Simmons. I wondered if these families were just neighbors by chance or knew each other before living there and had traveled together to Oklahoma. I concluded because James and Mercy lived in Muskogee prior to coming to Oilton, they could be eliminated from the theory they traveled together or knew each other.

Nancy Ellen and Charles Peterson

The Petersons on the census were Charles with his wife Nancy Ellen Simmons Peterson, who was James and Mercy's daughter. The Neighbors were John Henry and Ida Lee Thompson Neighbors. The Creek family was related on the Thompson side of the family. The Neighbors' daughter Mollie Catherine eventually married James and Mercy's son, Stephen.

Peterson Heritage Background

Born as Karl Axel Emil Persson in 1858, Charles registered for passage on October 19, 1879, and migrated to America from Sweden on a ship that was large enough to also carry a cattle

[Neighbors, Simmons and Peterson Family picture, taken shortly after wedding day of Stephen Boles Simmons and Mollie Catherine Neighbors]
Top Row: Left to right: *Ida Lee (Thompson) Neighbors and John Henry Neighbors, Mollie Catherine (Neighbors) Simmons and Stephen Boles Simmons, Charles Peterson and Nancy Ellen (Simmons) Peterson, Amanda (Peterson) Flynn;*
Middle Row: *John Emmett Neighbors, Mercy Elizabeth (Sutton) Simmons seated, John Wesley Peterson, Elva Pearl (Neighbors) German;*
Front Row: *Mable (Peterson) Riseling, Eva Faye (Neighbors) Newcomb*

barge. Information was provided to me by Bob and Margie Peterson, Charles' grandson. He traveled with Carl Olaffson, an uncle, and perhaps a sister, Eugenia Karolina. He carried with him all of his life savings. As many immigrants did when they arrived to make a new life, Karl changed his name. His parents were Per Johan Ollaffson and Christina Samuelsdotter but as he began his new life as an American, he became Charles Axil Peterson.

Charles was found on the 1880 Federal Census as living in Chicago, Cook County, Illinois with a household of other Swedes who may or may not have been related to him. They ranged from ages 22 to 34 and their names were all Peterson. He was living in Minneapolis, Minnesota, in 1885 and also there in 1895 records. It is not known whether Charles migrated into Iowa or Missouri where the Neighbors lived, but the first record of his residence in Oklahoma was 1897 on his marriage license.

According to the Homestead Act of 1862, Oklahoma Territory was opening and people were being offered 160 acres during that time. It is believed by family members that Charles was in search of the American dream. One could visualize some of these events that perhaps transpired as pioneers headed west, similar to the characters in a movie such as "Far and Away."

Black Gold, One of
Oklahoma's Greatest Resources

Twenty-two years her senior, Charles married Ellen Simmons in Jennings, Oklahoma, in 1897, shortly after her seventeenth birthday. It is not completely known or derived from family history if Charles knew about the drilling and discovery of oil in Oilton, Oklahoma, but he was listed as a farmer. Their first children, Amanda, Mable, and John, were born in that area. Their fourth child, Charles, often commented to me that he was not sure why he was the only Texan in the family, being born in Big Wells, Texas, in 1912. The family moved back to Oilton for Oscar's birth in 1914, the same year that Paul Emmett Simmons was born.

It has always been assumed Charles Sr. owned quite a bit of

land in Oilton or at least had access from land allotments to name an area in which they may have lived. At one time there was an area in Oilton referred to as Peterson Flats. If one travels

Streets in Oilton were named for
"Ellen" and "Charles" Peterson.

to that small community today, he or she would see some of the main streets in Oilton today, especially those close to the schools are named "Ellen," "Charles," and "Peterson."

Oklahoma Oilmen

Besides seeking a better future by farming or ranching, people were drawn to Oklahoma hoping to "strike it rich" with the fast-traveling news of success in drilling for oil. Cherokee and Choctaw Nations in Oklahoma had found oil on their lands before the white settlers arrived. The first commercial oil well was drilled in Bartlesville, 1897, the Nellie Johnstone #1. Billed as "the town that made Tulsa famous," Glenpool was the next area to discover oil in 1905. Wildcatter Tom Slick put Drumright on the map with Wheeler #1 in 1912, followed by drilling in an area along the Cimarron River in 1915, which was little more than a cotton patch, but caused the area to explode with growth.

Oilton, perhaps originally called Oil Town, was unique from the other towns that discovered oil because it was known as the roughest and toughest town in the oil field, not a place for the faint of heart. It was there the Peterson, Simmons, and Neighbors families began their relationships together.

After completing this chapter, I visited with Aunt Eva Faye Neighbors Newcomb's oldest son, John Edgar Newcomb. When I told him about my recent discoveries about Oilton, his reply was "I remember some things about Oil Town." The events that he mentioned helped identify pictures I had taken to Drumright Historical Society to glean some historical knowledge. John said his Grandpa John Henry Neighbors used his wagon and team of horses to help haul oil winch equipment and sometimes pulled other wagons and equipment out of the quicksand on the Cimarron River where they were drilling for oil.

Mable Peterson Riseling and Myrtle Moore Wade posing in their fur coats and hats

Tammy Posey, curator of Drumright Historical Museum referred me to her mother-in-law, Mrs. Frankie Posey, shared stories of photographers who traveled the oil field sites during that time to take pictures and sell them to the drillers and workers. She mentioned one such photographer who may have taken all or some of our family pictures was Benjamin Franklin Russell, better known as Ben Russell, called a "photographer with the soul of an artist."

It is believed the Petersons were involved in these oil fields oil, as well as Ellen's sister and brother-in-law, Jane and James Moore. They obviously prospered because some of the pictures I have seen in family albums of Ellen and Jane's older children, Mable and Myrtle, show them posing in fur coats and fashionable hats, a real luxury for the time.

From Oilton to Broken Arrow

Sometime in 1900 or shortly afterwards James Simmons, Mercy, and Stephen, the last child to have lived at home, traveled to Florida to stay for awhile because of James' health. These three posed in one family picture on the front porch of a cabin in Florida with a sawfish they landed on a fishing excursion. James seemed to have had an injury or illness of some kind. The extent of the illness has never been completely known. Rumor has it he may not have fully recovered from a gun shot wound when he was once ambushed from behind. It was common in that day for one to die of lead poisoning from a bullet that was not removed. Although it could have been from a hunting accident, the story seems more exciting to believe James may have been in a "shoot-out" at one time or another. However, ambushes during those times, could have been possible, but not necessarily associated with a gang of outlaws. After learning Oilton was the toughest area of the Oklahoma oil fields, it may be understandable James could in fact have been attacked from behind, most likely ambushed with robbery as motive. None of these possibilities has been ruled out.

The family of three returned from Florida to Broken Arrow, specifically the Fry community, southwest of town in the vicinity of 91st Street (Washington Street) and Mingo Road where James died. This information is according to an article in the

James, Mercy Simmons and youngest son,
Stephen Boles - ca. 1905

Broken Arrow Ledger dated March 16, 1905:

Uncle Jimmie Simmons died last Friday at the home of his brother John, near Fry, and was buried in the cemetery here on Saturday. Uncle Jimmie was one of the early settlers in this section of the country and resided here many years, going from here to Florida for his health where he remained about four years returning last fall. He was well known and highly respected by all the earlier citizens of this section of the country.

John Wesley and Clara Simmons were verified on Broken Arrow's first 1904 census report in the Fry community with his grandsons, William and Estil "Dutch" who were sons of one of his and Emily Jane's daughters. John Wesley died in 1912 in Wilburton, Oklahoma but is buried in White Church Cemetery, an historic cemetery located southwest of Broken Arrow.

Many other family members of Emily Jane Jackson's lived in Tulsa County during that time. One relative, James W. (Jim) Jackson was married to Sarah Sutton who was also related to Mercy Sutton and other Suttons in this area. Jim Jackson and his family lived in Tent City in Jenks, Oklahoma about 1907 until moving closer to the Broken Arrow area. Their daughter Belle Jackson married Frank Simmons and had children Pearl and Dee, who are related to the Sloan, Geneva and Lofton families in the Broken Arrow and Coweta areas. Although I didn't know some of these family connections in earlier years, Daddy and Mother were well-acquainted with the Geneva family, especially Wilma Geneva who worked at the Wagoner County Election Board for many years.

Other Simmons' Migrate to Broken Arrow

E.L. (Elmer Louis) "Mike" Simmons was on our school board in Broken Arrow during the 1950s and 1960s. His parents were James Thomas Simmons and Martha Ida Turner who had moved to this area from Muskogee. Mike was married to Florence McManus and fathered Martha, Louise and Victor.

Later Mike married Dorothy Cochran Davis and fathered two more children, Sue Ann Simmons Scace and Mike Simmons who were classmates, but also second cousins to the contemporary Simmons children. Mike and Dorothy were not only cousins of my dad, but good friends with him through the years. Daddy interacted a lot with both of them from school board business to city business where Dorothy was the City Clerk.

Mike's daughter Sue Ann and granddaughter Amy Morris Marcoux were able to attend our 100th year celebration reception for Daddy in November, 2014. Sue Ann's sister and Amy's mother, Louise Simmons Morris was good friends with Mother. They visited quite often about genealogy and their individual progress. Louise submitted a story which was published in a Broken Arrow Historical Society newsletter in October, 1990:

Martha Ida (Turner) and James Simmons are shown with their children, left--Clarence; standing in back--James Thomas; center front--Elmer Louis (Mike). Photo was taken about 1900.

- Courtesy of Broken Arrow Historical Museum - Broken Arrow, Oklahoma.

Simmons Family - Early Pioneers from Kansas

"My grandfather, James Thomas Simmons was born near Greeley, Kansas, on September 13, 1863. He died in October 2,1933 in Oklahoma City, and is buried in

Park Grove Cemetery, Broken Arrow.

He moved to Muskogee, Indian Territory, where he met and married my grandmother, Martha Ida Turner. She was born in Tarrant County, Texas...

My grandparents moved to Elam, in 1901. They crossed the Arkansas River on the ice by wagon. When the settlement of Elam moved to Broken Arrow, my grandparents also moved...

My grandfather's brother and wife, Joseph Sylvester and Elizabeth operated the Vena Hotel in Broken Arrow and it was later operated by my grandparents. My mother came from Campbell, Missouri and worked at the hotel where she met my father, Elmer Louis "Mike" Simmons. They were married on January 23, 1921.

When my father was a teenager, he lived in the big yellow house across the street to the north from IGA, which is now Metro Bank. Dad said an outlaw gang used to come to their house to water their horses..."

Kentucky Colonel Hotel
■ Courtesy of Broken Arrow Historical Museum - Broken Arrow, Oklahoma.

Simmons Cottage Hotel

▪ Courtesy of Broken Arrow Historical Museum - Broken Arrow, Oklahoma.

Some Simmons families were in the restaurant, boarding house and hotel businesses. The first hotel in Broken Arrow which is one that almost everyone is familiar with is the Kentucky Colonel Hotel. It was built in 1903 and 1904 by Colonel G.W. Gist of Lexington, Kentucky and owned by J.S. (Joseph Sylvester) Simmons. In 1916, under new ownership, the name changed to the Charles Hotel and then renamed Broken Arrow Hotel.

John Milton 'Tobe' and Daisy Simmons' Family

J.S. and Elizabeth Simmons also operated Hotel Vena, located at 202 West Dallas but perhaps did not own it. This hotel underwent several name changes such as Francis Hotel and Mains Hotel but referred to and remembered mostly nowadays as "the old Jacob boarding house".

Located on Main Street the Simmons Cottage was also one of Broken Arrow's first hotels and was owned by one of James' brother, John Milton "Tobe" and his wife Daisy Frances Hughes Simmons. It was highlighted on a 1908 postcard along with Hotel Estell. Charles and Hazel Hoag Peterson told me a little about Tobe as they remembered him. Besides other Simmons families, Tobe and Daisy also lived in the Fry Community on a farm close to 91st Street and Mingo.

Petersons are Broken Arrow Bound

During those booming oil years in the Oilton area, many prospered and became quite wealthy. As more oil field workers and people with a "get rich quick" attitude flocked to Oilton, other businesses came to gladly accommodate them in assisting the workers at spending their money. These businesses were bars, dance halls and pool parlors. As one vice begets another, before long there was crime and hotels catered to ladies of the evening. This type of environment was not conducive to rearing a moral family.

Because parents are always seeking the best environments and lifestyles for their children, our three families may have felt the same way. Between 1915 and 1920, there were drastic changes in Oilton's population. One young woman by the name of Lora Davis Dentler was a freshman in a class of 39 students in 1916. She recalled as a senior in 1920 she was school editor of the yearbook and her class consisted of only one other classmate. All other families had moved away.

A Young Construction Workers' Destiny

However, there was a young highly-skilled construction worker in town, obviously talented because his services were always in demand. His name was Laurence L. (Scottie) Scott. He once had a weakness for Scotch and Irish whiskey, but once he gave up his drinking, he became well-known in the area as a self-proclaimed untaught evangelist. It is said he already had a knack for attracting people and began reading his Bible and prayed he would have success and talent.

The Scotch-Irish heritage from the Sutton link may have influenced Ellen Simmons Peterson and compelled her and Charles to pursue more desirable educational opportunities instead of associating with this rough stock of people. Their second oldest daughter would have graduated in 1920 with Lora, but instead graduated from high school in Broken Arrow, Oklahoma. There were other Suttons who graduated with Mable and were cousins from Mercy Elizabeth's lineage.

Scottie was successful in Drumright so in 1917 people from Oilton asked him to come preach there. One of his favorite things was to go directly into the bars and saloons and invite the patrons to his revivals. He was very successful and most people were "flabbergasted" at his boldness. Early pioneers and citizens in the Oilton area have no doubt passed his stories down to their children, grandchildren and other people in the community because he helped to turn the town around. He was getting ready to move away and was asked to go to upstairs at a rooming house and help to minister to one of their girls who had just lost a baby. He did so. She and other girls at this brothel were converted to Christianity. Another amazing story is how he turned a house of ill-repute into a hospital and helped to eradicate the influenza in Oilton during an epidemic.

Although the Petersons did not stay to see people change and the small little town of Oilton make a turn around, it is a quiet, nice clean community today with courteous respectable people living there.

Ellen and Charles Peterson with Mable and Amanda

Aunt Jane and Aunt Ellen

Daddy and Mother were very close to our Aunt Jane and Aunt Ellen, James and Mercy's daughters. Before I knew them, Jane and James Moore moved to the Oklahoma City area and began a boarding house there. Stephen's oldest son James Henry lived with them while he attended and finished school at Foster High School. Apparently they had moved to Mead, Oklahoma because that is where James Moore died in 1935. My dad mentioned in an interview he helped Aunt Jane on their farm around that time.

During the 1940s and 1950s, Jane Moore was living in the Broken Arrow area, as was Ellen. The Petersons remained in Broken Arrow and the Tulsa area, where they reared children and grandchildren until their deaths on or close to their farm located near the intersection of the southeast corner of 91st (Washington Street) and Garnett Road, west of Broken Arrow. These families were known and well-respected in the community. The Peterson family was actually very instrumentally involved in the success of Stephen and Mollie's children, particularly Paul Emmett Simmons.

Charles and Ellen's children did not stray very far from their hometowns. Although their grandchildren may have lived a few other places, they generally came back to their roots in the Broken Arrow area, most settling no farther than Tulsa, Rogers or Wagoner Counties in their latter years.

Charles and Ellen Peterson's children:
Mable, Charlie, John, Oscar and Amanda

Amanda and Julius Flynn had no children. Mable and Lawrence Riseling lived mostly in the Sand Springs area with their family. John and Bernice Peterson lived in Broken Arrow. They had four children. Their son Bob and Margie Peterson owned and operated The Nut House in Claremore for a number of years. Their daughter Betty married Jimmy Stevenson, Jimmy's dad owned a car repair business just north of First National Bank on Main Street in Broken Arrow. At age 20, Jimmy began Arrow Cleaner; he was part-owner of Wardrobe Cleaners in the 1950s. He bought Yale Cleaners in January, 1959; it is still a family-owned business in the Tulsa area and the largest dry cleaner in Oklahoma. Charles, Jr. (Charlie) married Hazel Peterson after meeting her at one of the local hotel restaurants where she was working as a waitress. Charlie bought a market from Tracey Hunsecker, Sr. and began Warehouse Market. It was located in the same block as Arkansas Valley State Bank, just north of Nelson Ford Company, which is now part of the bank's property across the street from Broken Arrow Historical Museum. Charlie sold Warehouse Market in 1963 and that business is still operated in the Broken Arrow area. Oscar never married and was a farmer in Wagoner County, Oklahoma.

The Peterson family continues to have strong roots in the Broken Arrow area and northeastern Oklahoma. What may have begun as a humble beginning in the Oilton and Jennings area produced some strong and successful family members.

Warehouse Market, Broken Arrow, Oklahoma, ca. 1950's,
Charlie Peterson (center)

Having a similar but unique history of its own, the Neighbors family who were also in this area during the turn of the

20th Century had two of their youngest children born in Indian Territory, specifically Creek County. So there may have actually been other family members other than Paul Emmett Simmons who were born in that legendary log cabin in Oilton.

John Henry Neighbors, a "tin type" picture of a young cowboy in the Dakotas (about age 16)

Chapter 2
THE NEIGHBORS FAMILY MOVES WEST

With the Louisiana Purchase of 1803 and as Lewis and Clark completed their Journey of Discovery in 1806, people with a yearning for adventure and exploration began seeking that opportunity by moving west. It was important to me to first lay the foundation and research from which states our particular Simmons and Neighbors family lines originated, and the possible trails, routes and towns each traveled through to reach our present state of Oklahoma.

The previous generation of our Simmons clan hailed from Kentucky, while the Neighbors came from Iowa, further to the north. The Thompsons were in Ohio, but moved to Iowa, making it possible for that one family line to merge with the Neighbors.

Westward Ho!

Paul Emmett's maternal grandparents were John Henry Neighbors and Ida Lee Thompson. Both were born in 1872, one from Missouri, the other from Iowa. The living children of John Henry and Ida Lee's were Mollie Catherine (Mollie), Elva Pearl (Pearl), John Emmett (Emmett) and Eva Faye (Faye) Neighbors. Emmett and Faye were the only two of the children born in the Jennings, Oklahoma area. Emmett was born in Indian Territory with Faye born two years later in the same area, but under the name of our newest state, Oklahoma.

John Henry was born in Dean, Appanoose County, Iowa, which is on the northern border adjoining the state of Missouri. The Neighbors family may have lived in both these states during his childhood when the land in Missouri and Iowa was untamed and rugged.

John Edgar Newcomb, Faye Neighbors Newcomb's oldest son and one of Grandpa Neighbors' youngest grandchildren shared a story about John Henry walking home from school one day when he was about six years old. He was following a path through the woods that lay several miles between home and school when he was attacked by a wolverine. The only thing he had to defend himself with was his lunch pail; a one-gallon lard can with a wire handle. He yelled and hit the wolverine with the can until it finally ran off and left him alone.

The Apple Doesn't Fall from the Tree

John Henry's mother died when he was young. It was handed down by word of mouth when his father remarried, that he did not like his stepmother or perhaps just had a hard time adjusting. Maybe being intrigued by stories of the West, tales of "cowboys and Indians" or the Cavalry, John Henry left home at about the age of 12. It has been estimated that he joined up with a cattle outfit toward Dakota Territory in 1884. Five more years passed before North and South Dakota became states.

Recently as I was reading some interesting stories that were dictated from Paul Emmett's Grandpa Neighbors to John Newcomb, I realized that those tales sounded as if they could have been told by my own dad. They were stories of a young man venturing out on his own during the wild and hard pioneering days. Those same stories may have been related to Paul Emmett by Grandpa Neighbors, but he never recorded them as Paul's cousin John did. I could just imagine Paul wanting to follow in some of the same footsteps as his grandpa did.

When he was a cowboy in the Dakotas, John Henry as well

as other cowhands had bedrolls that were made of big pieces of canvas that he called a "tarpaulin" from which our contemporary word "tarp" is derived. It was covered with tar on one side to make it waterproof and his blankets were rolled inside. He slept outside on the ground and would sometimes wake up covered by up to two feet of snow. John Newcomb was impressed with his grandpa's ability to adapt quickly in learning survival skills. John may have thought that his grandpa was tougher and more mature than most boys the same age. When he first joined the cattle outfit, John Henry helped the cook and worked around the chuck wagon. When he was older he was assigned to care for the "remuda" which was the name for the horse herd. Each cowboy had two or three horses to ride throughout the day, so there were about fifty horses in the camp. Because there was no grain and only grass to eat, the horses tired easily, so the cowboys had to change horses two or three times a day. It was Grandpa's job to move the horses when the camp moved, which was often, and to catch each cowboy's "next" horse and have it in the camp when the rider came in to change horses. The remuda was corralled inside a pen made of a single rope suspended from poles. He must have been a pretty good roper to have lassoed, corralled and managed fifty horses in his teenage years. Since each cowboy rode more than one horse, matching horses with riders would have not been an easy chore.

Hearing Grandpa Neighbors' stories, John Edgar, like many youngsters caught up with "cowboy and Indian stories," asked if his grandpa had ever "shot an Indian". That provoked John Henry to share a truthful story about the Indians in the Dakotas. He told his grandson that sometimes Indians would come to the camp. They were hungry and looking for food for their families. They had very few clothes and were often wrapped only in a blanket for the coldest weather. The cow boss would give them a cow and the cook would give them whatever flour and salt that he could spare. John was very touched by his grandpa's obvious compassion for the plight of the Indians.

One day Grandpa Neighbors was out on the prairie, on horseback of course, when he came across a coyote he was able to chase down and rope. He dragged it back to camp and tied it to the chuck wagon since that was the only available hitching place and provided the only shade. When the cowboys would come in at noon they would get a drink of water from the water barrel then duck under the chuck wagon to get into the shade while they were waiting to eat. This day of course met the unhappy snarling coyote so they would immediately scoot right out again. At first they would be mad but then realize that another rider would be coming in and would do the very same thing—get a drink and head for the shade. At this point, they would watch from afar and wait for the fun to begin when their fellow cowboys ducked under the wagon. John was reminded that in those days out on the prairie, there was not much entertainment, so playing practical jokes on their cowpoke friends was a great treat.

Back Home to Settle Down and Marry

John Henry Neighbors had a lot of experiences for about six years before returning home to the Midwest. There he met Ida Lee Thompson, whose family had moved to the Chariton, Putnam County, Missouri area from Brown County, Ohio. They married in 1892. Their first child, a son named James Lester was born the next year, followed by Mollie Catherine, Paul Emmett's mother in 1895.

Perhaps always wanting to follow his adventurous side, John Henry was preparing to move his wife and two children to California

Ida Lee Thompson
Neighbors, ca. 1892

with Ida Lee's brother, Ed or to join them there. John Newcomb seemed to think the death of their son, little Lester affected their decision and deterred them from moving that far away. Having died from the croup, Lester was buried in Missouri. Pearl, another daughter, their third child was born in 1899. Somehow they decided to come to Oklahoma instead.

Neighbors Coming to Oklahoma from Missouri

John Newcomb told me that Grandpa Neighbors had a team of horses and a large wagon with a canvas cover similar to the type of Conestoga covered wagons but not as large. It was in that wagon that the Neighbors made their trip to Oklahoma. I did not know any of the details about when they left Missouri to come this direction, but remembered Grandma Mollie Simmons telling me a story of rats gnawing on her fingers in the back of the wagon at night on the trip. She showed me the marks she still bore from those scars.

I put together another piece of the puzzle as my cousin John told me that Grandpa Neighbors used his wagon and team of

Mollie Catherine
Neighbors, ca. 1898

horses without the covered part attached to help pull oil equipment out of the Cimarron River near Jennings and Oilton, Oklahoma. It was then I realized the pictures I had found in my Neighbors' files matched the descriptions of work being done in the oil fields, mostly in Oilton. So gradually this patchwork quilt continues to fit together.

Faye Remembers

Even though Faye was the youngest child of John and Ida Lee's, she was just as independent and headstrong as any of the others. She once told me about a picture that was made of her in front of C.W. Shoemake's Store when she was a young child. She had a vivid memory because she described her dress to me as a green wool or corduroy and couldn't have been barely more than two years old. The store was located close to the Cimarron River where people loaded to cross the ferry over to Jennings.

Faye and parents standing with Mr. and Mrs. C.W. Shoemake
Getting ready to cross the Cimarron River by ferry....'
at Jennings, Oklahoma ca. 1910

She was very excited to ride the ferry that day. She and her older brother were born in Jennings but her parents were on the Creek County census of Oilton in 1900. By 1920, the family was on the Hugo census. There are many more stories to tell about my Aunt Faye.

Grandma Neighbors Can Hold Her Own

As families often do, we traveled several times to Hugo to visit with our great-grandmother, Ida Lee. I could tell that Daddy enjoyed visiting with her. She was widowed in 1945, only about six months after my brother Chris was born. Although I mostly remember when I was between the ages of ten and fourteen years old, I never noticed what a tall and stately woman Grandma Neighbors was. She may have lost inches and became stooped in her latter years, but her height is obvious looking back at pictures of her now, especially compared with other family members, even Grandpa Neighbors.

My cousin JoAnn Simmons Smith and I recall her attempt to teach us how to knit or crochet, which neither of us retained. I remember eating rice with milk and cream for breakfast at her little house on 315 North "J" Street in Hugo, the house in which John Edgar and perhaps others were born.

I mostly recognized her pioneer spirit showing strong when she would show me the gopher skins she carefully kept wrapped in cellophane covers. At first I was intrigued but shocked at the thought of this loving grandmother trapping and killing gophers in her yard, then skinning them. But now knowing some of these hardy tales about her family makes sense. Their trapping skills were of necessity not just sport, but survival skills, which meant keeping warmer in the winter, when Ida Lee was a child.

She was also adept in handling a shotgun. She was approaching ninety years old when she was still shooting crows to keep them out of her yard. Unfortunately her eyesight was not as sharp as her mind. Much to her chagrin, one day she missed a crow but did not realize she had shot her telephone wire in two. She wondered why her telephone was not working, but quickly figured it out and reported it to be repaired.

More Stories about Ida Lee

John Newcomb not only shared antics of his grandpa, but told tales passed down from Ida Lee's family. The locations may have been in Ohio or more easterly, before the Thompsons traveled to the Midwest perhaps as early as the 1800's. These stories were about her side of the family.

When Grandma's grandmother was a small child she was riding behind her own mother on a horse, going through the woods to a neighbor's house several miles away. When the horse started to act up the woman looked behind them and found that a cougar was following closely. She reached around and picked up the child and pulled her into her lap, then let the horse have free rein to get away from the cat. When the men went back to hunt the cat they found a big dusty cougar paw print on the little dress the child had been sitting on behind the saddle. It had fallen to the ground when she was moved into her mother's lap.

Because John was in between my dad's age and mine, he had an opportunity to know his grandpa well and have many conversations with him. One could imagine our great-grandparents conveying the following story to John and his younger brother Jim in each their own version of what happened. John recalls another incident happening back in Missouri before coming to Oklahoma. He said Grandpa had a favorite dog he used to hunt raccoons among other things. One night he was out hunting when a big raccoon dragged the dog into a deep and swift river. Grandpa left his lantern on the riverbank and jumped into the river, although he couldn't swim, making a daring rescue because of his love for the dog. Apparently he saved the dog or the commotion scared the raccoon, but he himself obviously survived the ordeal. John may have heard that particular story repeated by his grandparents over and over, but was amused by Grandma's fussing and still scolding him for risking his own life since he did not even know how to swim!

Mollie, Pearl, Emmett, Faye,
Reverend J.H. and Ida Lee Neighbors

Of all the stories, John Edgar was mostly impressed with one that could have only been heard by observing a visionary. John said he and Grandpa were outside one day and saw the moon in full and clear view in a mid-morning sky. Grandpa said to John, "Men will go to the moon during your lifetime. You should live until at least the year 2000."

"How will they do it?" I asked.

He replied, "I don't know but they'll figure out a way." John Henry Neighbors was ahead of his time in thinking of future events and inventions, but he had no idea what technology was way ahead of him. In retrospect, not only did the event occur during his grandchildren's lifetimes but all four of his and Ida Lee's children were still living at the time of the first moon landing in 1969. John marveled at the fact his grandpa never attended school after the age of twelve but was obviously intelligent in other ways.

Ida Lee apparently had a strong personality which may have attracted her to her robust and adventuresome counterpart. They no doubt produced four children who were of hardy stock as well.

Mollie Catherine had a personality of a typical first-born although she was born as a second child. Mollie was around two years old when the family grieved over the death of her older brother, Lester. Whether by genes, by becoming the first-born or molding by her parents, Mollie exhibited the same strong personality from which her pioneering parents came and she in turn birthed Paul Emmett and his siblings most of whom had much the same nature, some being more verbal in their personalities than others. So, from that adventuresome cowboy pioneer spirit to the humor of enjoying practical jokes, the proverb that an apple doesn't fall far from the tree could be true or as one might say, "Those trees don't sling them apples!"

Paul Simmons on Black Beauty

Chapter 3
OUR SIMMONS' HERITAGE

As the Civil War came to an end in 1865 and with the completion of the Transcontinental Railroad in 1869, the descendants
of our American immigrant families began moving west for
various reasons which perhaps included that American dream.

Research and curiosity began with the discovery of James
Simmons' parents, James and Anna Whittington Simmons. Although they came from Kentucky, this family had eleven children, consisting of nine boys and only two daughters who were
born in different states. There has always been strong evidence
pointing to the fact many of the Simmons families who came
from these two parents moved often and were difficult to find
on census reports. Family members had good horsemanship
abilities, probably due to at least five of the nine Simmons sons
being soldiers in the Civil War.

One of James and Anna's sons was James. James' youngest
son was Stephen Boles Simmons. Paul Emmett Simmons' parents were Stephen Boles Simmons, born in 1885 in Tulsa, Indian Territory and Mollie Catherine Neighbors, born in 1895 in
Carollton County, Missouri. Rumor always had it that Mollie's
parents did not want her to marry Stephen, because of their age
difference. Also family members somehow seemed to get the
impression that Stephen was the unsettled cowboy type. Their
marriage license from Oswego, Kansas in April, 1911 gives both
their residences as Yale, Oklahoma. Both Stephen and Mollie
were living with their families in this area of Creek County in
1900. Mollie was less than sixteen years old when she and Stephen married. Stephen may have persuaded Mollie, a young

strong-willed young lady, to elope. It appears they applied for a license in Yale and traveled to Kansas to marry.

Faye Neighbors, James, Paul, Earl and Kathryn Simmons

Stephen and Mollie had four children, James Henry, Paul Emmett, Peter Earl and Ida Kathryn, born within their first eight years of marriage. Once they began having children, each was born almost two years apart, with dates ranging between November, 1912 and January, 1919, within slightly over six years. The two older boys were born in Oilton, Creek County, Oklahoma.

The earliest picture I have of Paul Emmett Simmons is sitting on a blanket in the yard when he was about six months old. On the back of the picture it states "Rock Hill" which is close to Hugo. It is not known as to whether they were just visiting the area after Paul was born or had moved because Earl their third son was born in Hugo, Oklahoma. They were back in the Tulsa area by 1920 where their only daughter was born.

Paul's paternal grandparents were James Simmons and Mercy Elizabeth Sutton, from Indiana and Kansas respectively. Paul was aware of his English and Scotch-Irish lineage, probably mostly from the Sutton family. My parents had often mentioned this respectful Sutton family in conjunction with conversations about family history and their knowledge of a whole area which is known by many people in southeast Kansas as "Sutton Valley". There was also discussion of questionable information about the Simmons clan, who hailed from various locations in the southern states and not as easy to research from their trail of relocating often.

Although Paul always enjoyed knowing where his roots began, he felt like it was much more important to know "where one was going than from where one had come".

Tryin' to Make a Living

During the rough and hard pioneering days of Oklahoma in the 1920s, having a wife and four children under eight years of age was not easy.

My dad had told me more than once his dad barely had a third grade education. I knew it was not uncommon for pioneer people or families without monetary means to be uneducated. I suppose I always assumed these families were just poor and could not afford to attend school, not because they traveled a lot or perhaps were in search of a better life by moving to their promised land.

Because our Uncle Earl was the last of Stephen and Mollie Simmons' children to pass away, he visited with most of his nieces and nephews often and shared several stories with us. As a vital link to the past, our Uncle Earl filled in the blanks as to the various places where the Simmons' lived in their early years.

Future "cousin reunions" that evolved from our wanting to know about our parents' rearing, was partly the reason research was begun. It revealed Stephen and Mollie moved several times during these early years. Changing jobs and moving frequently may have been a common thing at those times. Several of us had individual conversations and interviews with our Uncle Earl from time to time. Once he drove three of us to Tulsa and to various schools and addresses that he recalled as being the Simmons' residences.

In 1917 when Earl was about six months old, the Simmons

family moved back to the Tulsa area from Hugo. Earl recalled they lived in a variety of places, mostly on North Quaker, where they lived when he attended kindergarten at Lowell Elementary.

While in Tulsa Mollie and Stephen's youngest child, Kathryn was born in 1919. The federal census showed the family living in Tulsa in 1920 when Kathryn was 1 year old. The family lived in the same area in about 1921 when the Tulsa race riots began. Earl told the cousins his dad drove a truck that hauled dead bodies of black people out of town during that tragic time. He did not expound on the subject, nor did he speculate. Those days were hard times for everyone, so no matter which side of the fence Stephen was on, he may have felt "a job was a job" and saw the need for a driver.

Men working in the railroad yard,
Stephen B. Simmons squatting in front, ca. 1920

During the 1920's after World War I had ended and when our

national economy was weakened, most jobs in this area were not plentiful. Stephen and Mollie were living at 727 N. Quaker Avenue as verified in a 1922 Tulsa address directory at the Oklahoma Historical Center. They were listed as Stephen B. and Mollie. It also stated he was the foreman at Prairie Oil and Gas Company. Although I have no details to support the information, a family picture of Stephen posing with other men at work. It looked as if it was a railroad yard in Tulsa. Working for the railroad was a good job at the time. MK & T passengers were enjoying a newly constructed train running through Broken Arrow from Muskogee, Tulsa and on to Oklahoma City.

The Quiet Humorous One

Earl enjoyed telling a favorite story about Belva Lester, his kindergarten teacher when he was five years old in 1921. Belva was a unique and special lady whose family is well known in Broken Arrow and Tulsa areas. Not wanting to appear older than she was, Belva always corrected Earl especially when he related the story to others in her presence. She reminded him that she was only 16 years old and they allowed young ladies to teach school while they were still working on their college degrees at the time. Mrs. Lester was originally from the Dakotas and came here to attend Kendall College its name prior to becoming to University of Tulsa. She and her husband, Jim met in Tulsa because they lived in the same apartment building. Our family knew them from First Methodist Church growing up. They were a family of all boys: Jim, Tom, Pat, Bill, Joe, Jeff and Mike, who have almost all been in law enforcement, the medical field and or community service. Jim and Belva far exceeded normal standards as parents. Belva started young in helping to educate Earl.

Out on the Lease

Simmons kids 'out on the lease' bundled up for Winter

Perhaps after they moved from North Quaker a little later in 1922 or 1923, when the children were about four, six, eight and ten, they lived on an oil lease northwest of Peoria and Mohawk where Stephen did maintenance on oil wells. Their house had gas but no electricity or running water. During this time the children attended school at Turley. Earl remembered a tractor wheel fell on him about this time.

There is picture of the Simmons children bundled up on a cold winter day posing together with the words "out on the lease" on the back of it.

I grew up understanding the term "out on the lease" because it not only is a common term used in Oklahoma, but many people have tried drilling for oil at least once. Our dad had a few oil leases of his own at various times.

Times of Innocence

There were times I would question my dad's authenticity of his many stories because he liked to joke and tease so much. I often would really doubt his giving me correct information about the ages of the boys at certain events. One time he told me James and he would go to the store for their mother to buy groceries by pulling a wagon, sometimes even before they were school age. That seemed to be an incredible story until I found a grocery ticket in a box of mementos. The ticket was signed by

James one time when he bought lard, flour, sugar and such. It was dated 1919; he was age 7.

Children have a way of being resilient and inventing their own fun and entertainment. My dad had a way with words, liked to say tongue twisters, and tell stories that required an excellent memory to regurgitate rhymes and riddles. During a time when the Simmons children were young, they had a Collie dog. Paul named her Polly. She would run under a cup of water as he poured it out onto her head. So he added to her name by calling her Polly-Woggum, Soak 'em Collie.

Earl, Paul, and James Simmons

Somewhere he had heard it was not good luck to change your dog's name, so as he thought of other unique names and phrases, he would just add to her name. He had finally added so many phrases to her original name it would take awhile for him to call her. Polly's name ended up being: Polly Woggum, Soak 'em Collie, Mary Ann, Fluitty Pruitt, Flip Willy Chip Lillie, California Livingston Avenue.

Impressionable

Occasionally I remember stories that were very impressionable to my dad. One in particular was the first time he heard a radio. His family was listening to a radio while sitting on a quilt in the yard during the summer of 1923. That was not only an exciting event in itself, but suddenly a shooting star darted across the sky. His grandmother commented, "A shooting star is a sign that someone famous just died." True or not, the next day, it was announced that President Warren G. Harding had suddenly passed away.

Our dad always reminded us to be grateful for what we had. He recalled one year when they were young, they had real candles alit on their Christmas tree. As one may have guessed, one candle tipped over and set the entire tree on fire. Presents were already under the tree and the fire burned up everything so they had no gifts that year for Christmas.

Another time he remembered a story about not wasting what one had. He told a story about how he and James were walking home from the store with a bag of beans to plant for spring. The playful boys began tossing the bag back and forth to each other when the bag finally split open and spilled out all over the dirt road. It was not easy to gather up what had been lost and a more meaningful lesson to them which would eventually affect their crop production.

It's all in a Name

Paul and Earl's parents may have purposely decid-

Paul, Charlie, James, Earl and Oscar - Simmons and Peterson boys in sombreros

ed to give these two boys names that bore the same initials. Or it could have been purely coincidental. One day they wanted to trade names. Their Aunt Pearl was married to Peter (Pete) German, for whom Earl may have been named. In playing, the boys became Peter Paul and Emmett Earl. In an interview, Paul referred to it as just a "secret between the two boys." So when the name Peter was shortened to Pete, it may have been the first time reference was given to his nickname. I believe Paul was quite fond of his Aunt Pearl and his Uncle Pete German, so it wouldn't have been surprising if he had wanted to be called Pete because of a favorite uncle. Years later, Aunt Pearl's daughter, Cora Lee German Green told me Paul was about five years old when Pearl and Pete got married and cried when they went on their honeymoon because he wanted to go with them.

But as legal names will follow people, Peter Earl Simmons' did. Earl worked at the downtown Tulsa Post Office after World War II. Earl actually became known as Peter, but shortened it to Pete at the post office during those many years until his retirement.

Give Me That Old Time Religion

Several documented conversations with our Uncle Earl lead us to particular conclusions. A few of the dates and names are different, but close enough to make sense and follow the trail of events and various addresses where this young family lived.

The most influential relationship that Mollie seemed to have was a neighbor by the name of Mrs. Reichord. They were neighbors at the location when they lived near the oil lease on North Peoria Street in Turley. As one could readily visualize these neighbor ladies visiting across the fence as they perhaps hung out their laundry. As ladies often do, Mrs. Reichord and Mollie probably talked about many different subjects, one of which was religion. Because of Mollie's rearing and background, it was perhaps a subject she felt she knew something about.

As history has shown us, after each major war or upheaval in the United States, it is followed by a spiritual awakening and revival. The famous revival of Azusa Street in Los Angeles, California, occurred just after the turn of the century. It began with a spark of desire for spiritual renewal born out of hours, days and months of prayer preceding a huge revival fire across the nation. It moved from the Topeka, Kansas area and spilled over to the Oklahoma and Arkansas areas, in inner cities as well as rural regions. Many people were rejected by their home churches and denominations so they resorted to meeting in outlying areas away from the cities, in brush arbors.

*Paul and his family attended the Raymond T. Richey Revival,
April, 1923 Tulsa, Oklahoma*
▪ Article/Photo used by Permission - Tulsa World - Tulsa, Oklahoma.

As in other wars in American history, a spiritual revival followed World War I. When there seems to be a disheartened feeling after a war that has devastated a nation, lost family members, weakened an economy and having experienced a falling away of people disillusioned by religion, there is always a remnant of people who operate in a spirit of hope. Revivals do not happen by coincidence. This remnant of hardy Americans had strong constitutions of conscience and spirituality with a glimmer of hope our country could regain its original intents. Tulsa was not unlike any other city in the southwest with strong religious roots.

Raymond T. Richey, a well-known evangelist of the time visited the Tulsa and Oklahoma City area during the spring of 1923. He erected a tent in Tulsa and held some revival meetings. One such meeting was held in April of 1923. Years later when I heard about this era of spiritual renewal in Tulsa, I asked Uncle Earl if he recalled attending such a revival meeting. Much to my surprise, he did! Sitting in his home on North Birch in Broken Arrow, he shared his recollection of this memory as a second grade child would recall the events of the evening. I was amused but not surprised as he smiled and told me the main thing he remembered about that event was the trombone player. It made perfect sense this seven year old child would be drawn to the music in a church service as he was many years later when he married a music teacher. Could it be God placed that love for music in his heart even as a child?

I am not a real skeptic, but like to research information to find facts to back up possible historical events. Indeed I found the Tulsa World carried a full week of articles about several revival meetings Raymond T. Richey held in the Oklahoma area, some of which were Tulsa. In reading his autobiography, I discovered Richey's brother was an accomplished trombone player and lead the worship music during these services.

As difficult as life may have been, perhaps these church services brought joy and conviction to the hearts of many, even to the hearts of these four children and their parents and neighbors.

Mission Trip

Earl recalled fairly well the places their family lived, their addresses and schools they attended. In 1925-26, Earl was in the fourth and fifth grades and attended Lowell School. They lived at 1715 E. Jasper. In 1926 they moved to 112 S. Lewis when he was ten and attended Whittier School in the fifth grade.

During the summer of 1927 before his sixth grade in school, Earl recalled his mother and Mrs. Reichord took their children to California, Missouri on a mission trip. Mrs. Reichord may have had relatives in Missouri but it may be unknown why they chose that area. Earl remembered they rode to and from Missouri in back of a trailer. Mollie did housekeeping and perhaps some cooking for a butcher and his family while in this small town of California. They lived in many places in town. Rent was low, but so were wages. As Earl recalled, they lived in six different houses. They had to move often, because they could not pay the rent. It is believed, while they were there, they were trying to establish a church. They stayed most of the summer. Nothing has ever been mentioned about "a Mr. Reichords," and it is not entirely known if Stephen traveled with them or joined the family later, but he did live in California, Missouri part of the time.

These two ladies may have had special times together, as they discussed religious issues that opened conversations of Bible lessons that they may have learned as youngsters. In Mollie it may have sparked a flame of an earlier conversion, attempting to fill a void or a yearning that was never completely fulfilled.

Without knowing much about their plans and relationship, they may have felt as if they could do more with their lives, but rather were stuck in a rut. They may have convinced themselves that they were only housewives, cooking, cleaning, scrubbing and perhaps in an unfulfilled life of poverty and not appreciated instead of one of glamour or destiny.

No matter what the motivation was and not having privy to their conversations and plans, some of their decisions and actions affected their families, the stability of their children's lives and their own destinies that were not realized until years later.

Sign reads:
"California, Missouri old-fashioned Revival Meeting"

John Emmett Neighbors
in World War I U.S. Army (Cavalry) uniform

Chapter 4
PREACHER OR OUTLAW

The legend continued as I inquired about whether or not it was true—was Paul Emmett REALLY named after one of the infamous Doolin or Dalton family members? Finally, as an adult, I asked my dad if it was true he was really named AFTER one of the outlaws. His answer, in his typical smirky humor was "Well, I wasn't named BEFORE him." He finally told me he was named for his uncle, John Emmett Neighbors, John Henry's only living son. He seemed to think Emmett was named for one of the Dalton gang, namely Emmett Dalton.

So, I still discounted it was just totally a made-up story, and had nothing to do with knowing or being related to these outlaws. Maybe Pete was just spinning one of his many yarns of the old west. However, in the late 1980's, I had an opportunity to renew an acquaintance of my Great Aunt, Eva Faye Neighbors Newcomb, the youngest daughter of John Henry Neighbors. Faye's son, John Newcomb is the one who took the time to record Grandpa Neighbors' Wild West stories. Aunt Faye shed a whole new light on the mystery of the legend.

Being inquisitive, I asked Faye if she knew anything about the story. When she replied, "Of course I do," I could hardly believe I was about to learn another version. This time, it seemed a great deal more credible. Eva Faye told me her dad, John Henry was intrigued by Emmett Dalton's autobiography and his experience as the lone survivor in the shootout that killed all the other Dalton brothers in Kansas. He penned most of his story from a Federal Penitentiary in Leavenworth, Kansas. Emmett Dalton, a hardened criminal, was converted to Christianity while in prison.

Being impressed with Dalton's life-changing experience, John Henry named his own son John Emmett in 1901, "after" Emmett Dalton, thus allowing the legend to come full circle and clarifying it into factual information. Apparently, John Henry Neighbors was so influenced by Dalton's autobiography in writing the pros and cons of outlaws and lawmen and his perspective of the difference between good and evil, he was eventually lead into the ministry himself. Faye wrote at the top of one of her family documents that her father "was called into the ministry when she was a baby," which may have been in about 1908. Aunt Faye was a true historian and constantly in search of the truth, as I was.

Ida Lee and Rev. John Henry (J.H.) Neighbors on their way to church

Reverend J.H. Neighbors became a Methodist pastor circuit rider in the Kiamichi Mountains of southeastern Oklahoma, in the rural area of Hugo and surrounding small towns. Rock Hill, Grant and Cloudy were three of the small rural areas where the family lived while he traveled. Many of the Thompson family, Ida Lee's parents and brothers lived in Cloudy. I have been told that there are still many Thompsons in areas of southern Oklahoma. When Paul was about 10 years old, he occasionally rode with his Grandpa Neighbors from town to town in his 1924

Ford Tourister. He was an impressionable and sensitive young man who heard his grandpa minister The Gospel of Jesus Christ to the people in these small Oklahoma towns who didn't have a regular preacher of their own. It was so influential to young Paul, it also became a life-changing experience. It was one I wasn't aware of until many years later when Daddy told me he wanted to be a preacher when he grew up. At the writing of this book, I began to wonder what conversations young Paul had with this special grandpa while traveling the back roads of these Oklahoma hills, and if they ever talked about Raymond T. Richey coming to Tulsa in April of that previous year.

Double Dose of Bible-believing

Although most "church stories" would probably be told from the Neighbors' side of the family, Paul's dad Stephen had a spiritual nature. My dad once related a story to me about a time when he was also about 10 years old. He said he went to his dad and showed him a wart on his hand. There is not much detail or information about the story, other than the fact Stephen just placed a handkerchief over the wart on Paul's hand and spoke a silent prayer. After he took the handkerchief off his hand, the wart was gone. It was actually years later my dad told me this story. I didn't think to ask more detail. I often wondered more about the spiritual side of Grandpa Simmons' life.

I just thought of him as a cowboy when he was younger. I believe I must have had that opinion mainly because my dad told me his dad taught him how to remember the four gospels: "Matthew, Mark, Luke and John—saddle my horse and I'll be gone."

One may wonder as I have what kind of relationship Stephen had with his father-in-law. In their own ways, both of these two former cowboys — Stephen Simmons and Grandpa J.H. Neighbors had strong influences on young Paul.

Mercy Elizabeth Sutton Simmons ca. 1924

Chapter 5
THE TRAGEDIES OF 1924

Sometimes people can pinpoint exact situations in their lives which make lasting impressions and possibly altering their thinking permanently—for good or bad. Paul Simmons had at least two life-changing events that affected him in negative ways in 1924.

His grandmother, Mercy Elizabeth Sutton Simmons, James' widow, was accidentally poisoned when she mistakenly drank rat poison instead of bicarbonate of soda for an upset stomach during the night. At the time of the accident she was visiting her other son, John Wesley and wife Clara Toothman Simmons, Stephen's older brother in New Mexico. Daddy remembered it being a difficult time, as a ten-year-old boy, walking from the funeral parlor which was on the second story above one of the businesses on Main Street in Broken Arrow all the way to Park Grove Cemetery on a cold and rainy day. As was the custom in those days, the family walked behind the wagon as it trudged through the mud.

The year 1924 was devastating in more than one way to the young Simmons family. Daddy's parents may not have divorced immediately, but at least began having difficulty during that year. Divorce was an event that was almost unheard of in those days. Not any details have been known because the four children did not talk about it as they became adults and had children of their own. The information I knew was very sketchy at best. Both these tragic events were devastating to the Simmons family. The two older children may have remembered more about these devastating events than the younger ones, but all of the children were obviously affected, especially the turmoil of their parent's marriage.

The Tragedy of Divorce

During the 1920's it was very uncommon for couples to divorce. It can affect each family member differently, but the devastation can last a lifetime. Based on individual perceptions, each child had their own thoughts about the divorce of their parents and reacted in different ways. While one child may express anger openly, another may internalize his or her pain and resentment. It is often common for a child to wonder why. But in fact, only Stephen and Mollie themselves knew the reasons why. Since divorce is more prevalent in today's society, most people would conclude though the married couple is the closest to the situation, even they could have wrong perceptions about their own relationship.

Stephen and Mollie often were reported as living together during these difficult years, perhaps after separating even before filing the initial divorce. That may have indicated they made several attempts to reconcile their differences. At least that would be the thinking of an optimist. Marital trouble for Stephen and Mollie may have started around 1924, but their divorce was apparently final in 1928.

Early Years with the Neighbors

I had always been given the impression my Grandma Mollie was rebellious and married against her parents' wishes. Not having grown up as a "preacher's kid", I cannot speak from that perspective, but I have concluded her parents adhered to a strict policy of discipline. Mollie could have also been very challenging as a child and adolescent with a strong will as well.

Lines Are Drawn in the Sand

When a divorce occurs, lines are drawn, sides are taken, hairs are split and people choose to take on the "Hatfield and McCoy" syndrome, which can result in more family difficulty, because there are always more facts in the situation than meets the eye. No one knows all the facts in a relationship except the two primary ones involved. No matter the "he said, she said" events, each person shares conversations from his or her perspective and may willingly or unwittingly slant the details in the way they want it to be perceived.

From that point, the division is begun, the disunity occurs and the disharmony continues, sometimes lasting through many generations. Unforgiveness and a root of bitterness can affect everyone in the family, justified or not.

Putting the Puzzle Together

About 2004, the grandchildren of Stephen and Mollie decided to begin planning reunions so these first cousins could get to know each other better. Most family reunions focus on picnics, renewing acquaintances, and reminiscing of their friendships during their childhoods. For our family, we met to "piece together" where each of their parents lived growing up, with whom they lived, and which ones lived together in the same household during specific years. Thankfully, our Uncle Earl was still living during the beginning of our Simmons family reunions, and he understood the interest the cousins had. He helped by documenting most places he attended school as was described in a previous chapter. The other children may or may not have lived in the same town he did.

Growing up in the Depression Times

Instead of returning to Tulsa in the fall of 1927 when Earl would have been ready for the sixth grade, the young Simmons family moved to Elston, Missouri. The children attended a one-room school. That year the school offered fifth and seventh grade classes. The following year was when they would have been teaching the sixth and eighth grade. Because the teachers in the small school felt Earl was not advanced enough for the seventh grade, they put him back into the fifth grade.

During the time Mollie and Mrs. Reichord were in California, Missouri, they met the Williams family. Whether in Tulsa or Missouri, apparently Mollie became romantically involved with Tom Williams. At some point Stephen moved to California, Missouri and went into business with Tom Williams' brother, who had a small coal mine. On several different occasions and in more than one conversation, Earl expressed he did not understand how his Dad could accept the situation the family found themselves in, especially the choices Mollie made. After experiencing a cave-in, it was reported Stephen decided that was not "the way he wanted to live, nor die" and made the decision to move back to Tulsa. It was at this time the couple divorced. Mollie married Tom Williams in 1928. The newly created family which included Tom and Mollie Williams and the four Simmons children— James, Paul, Earl and Kathryn— moved to Kansas City to Tom's sister's house, then to Harrisonville.

James and Paul were almost sixteen and fourteen respectively and most likely were resentful of Tom as their step-father. I remembered a conversation I had with Daddy about Tom several years later. He told me Tom tried to whip him once with a razor strap. He grabbed the strap out of Tom's hand and told Tom if he ever laid another hand on him, he would kill him. When Daddy told me that story, he also shared with me Tom was killed in a car accident a few years after that incident happened. Daddy told me he felt a great deal of guilt when Tom died, as if he had wished it upon him. James and Paul returned to Oklahoma soon after their Dad left.

During the time Mollie and the younger children lived in Missouri with Tom, they were exposed to making and selling moonshine. When I heard this story, I wondered if that was really the path Mollie would have chosen had she been able to predict her future.

I also began wondering if my dad, young Paul ever reflected back on the good experiences of traveling from town to town in the 1924 Ford Tourister, listening and learning as Grandpa Neighbors shared the Gospel the same year tragic events interrupted his childhood. Or did he feel as if God let him down with his grandmother's death and his parents'marital trouble?

"Picture of Happiness" 1924 Ford Tourister,
On the road to New Mexico and Arizona (J.H. & Stephen)

Because the family detectives have examined pictures and compared stories handed down from parents and confirmed by census reports, they have been able to piece back together the history behind the lives of at least six people, Stephen and Mollie Simmons and their four children— James Henry, Paul Emmett, Peter Earl and Ida Kathryn— in my case, one in particular— Paul Emmett .

"Paul E. Simmons,
Senior picture in 1932 Tulsa Central High School
Yearbook Caption:
"A likable chap who possesses pluck and ambition and a fighting spirit."

Chapter 6
SIMMONS ARE SURVIVORS

Although the main focus of this book is about Paul E. Simmons, part of his success and survival is due to the cohesiveness of his family ties, especially with his siblings. Each sibling has his and her own amazing stories of survival, coping and thriving. This common bond no doubt helped each one become dependent on one another while retaining a sense of independence.

Paul and James moved back to Broken Arrow shortly after their mother's marriage to Tom Williams in 1928. I knew Daddy lived in Broken Arrow his eighth and ninth grade years in high school because he told me and from seeing his picture in the freshman class of the Broken Arrow High School 1929 yearbook. I matched that information with the conversation he did in an interview. He said in the interview he recalled having to borrow clothes for his eighth grade graduation because he did not have anything decent to wear. Daddy also said in an interview and records show they both the boys lived with the Petersons in 1928 and 1929.

Earl recalled in his memoirs the Stock Market crashed in 1929 less than two months before he was thirteen which changed the economic situation of our nation. The following year, Earl had his eighth grade graduation at the country school in the little town of California.

Methodist Heritage returns

He also told me about his ninth grade Sunday school classroom at the First Methodist Church. His good friend was Amos Mizell.

First Methodist Church, built in 1924.
Pete and Amos Mizell formed 'Gideon's Army' in 1928.
He later returned to teach Wesley Sunday School class.

Daddy told me they called themselves "Gideon's Army", which may have been a club they formed. He said their Sunday school classroom was a small room which became the pastor's study in the 1960's.

In visiting with Howard Fisher, he told me Amos' father worked for Field's Bakery in the 1930's. Field's daughter, Dorothy was close to the ages of James and Paul and attended school with them. He reminded me when Amos grew to adulthood, he worked at Hunsecker's Dry Goods Store. Even as a man of over 90 years old, Howard had a remarkable memory. He told me the Mizell family lived in the 400 block of West Broadway. Later Amos Mizell and his family moved to Coweta, where he ran a business and was well known there.

Broken Arrow's First Methodist Church, located at College and Main Street was a landmark known for its tall white columns and stairs in the front. It had been built in 1924 and was a familiar spot for Vacation Bible School photographs, especially throughout the 1950's. It is not uncommon for Broken Arrow residents to still have one or more of those pictures in a family album. The combined churches that participated in those VBS programs were Methodist, Presbyterian and Christian, which all met within a block of each other from Main Street and College to Ash Street. The photographer was O.T. (Andy) Anderson. It was an unfortunate time in the late 1970's for the congregation to suffer the loss of this regal and historical structure when it burned down. Many Broken Arrow families during that time had been charter members of the church.

Field's Bakery, owned by Dorothy Field's parents.
Amos Mizell's father worked for them.
* Courtesy Broken Arrow Historical Museum - Broken Arrow, Oklahoma

Grateful to the Petersons

During at least part of Paul's short-lived 1928 and 1929 school career in Broken Arrow, he first lived with Steve's sister's family, Ellen and Charles Peterson. The Petersons had established their residence in Broken Arrow prior to Mable's graduation in

1920. Once Paul and James moved in with their dad, the exact times have not been determined where Stephen and the boys lived. The Peterson family farm was located on the south side of 91st Street close to Garnett. After moving from the Oilton area, Charles Peterson owned several acres of land in this area.

VBS (Vacation Bible School) on the steps of First Methodist Church at College and Main ca. mid-1950's
*Courtesy of O.T. "Andy" Anderson

Paul recalls he was
Broken Arrow's first paperboy.

I somehow got involved with the paper man in Broken Arrow. He had the contracts to throw all the Tulsa Tribunes in Broken Arrow. I threw the paper day and night from the running board of a 1928 Dodge Roadster. Ironically, I helped put the Tribune out of business many years later. I threw papers that first year and I stayed with my aunt and uncle then moved in with my dad when he had a place for me in Tulsa. I would go back to Broken Arrow on the weekends to throw the paper and lived on the edge of town with the Petersons.

"James and Paul Simmons enjoyed visiting with their Grandma Neighbors in Hugo" ca. 1929

Daddy was disappointed when he finally had to move from Broken Arrow to live in Tulsa with his dad. He expressed the main disappointment to moving was not being able to graduate from Broken Arrow. Another family allowed their son to ride a city bus to Tulsa. Daddy's perception was the friend changed schools in order to graduate from a more well-known town. Daddy just longed to stay in his beloved hometown, where he may have felt more family connection and security by remaining with the Petersons.

There were many underground springs in Broken Arrow in the early days and Daddy would tell a story about how he would take the horses into town, or at least to a spring to water them. It is undetermined where the watering spot was, but he enjoyed running alongside the horses as they trotted to their destination. It would not be unusual to visualize Daddy running to do his chores, as he was often seen running down Main Street later as a young attorney.

Tulsa Central High School

Originally Steve Simmons lived in West Tulsa when Daddy went to live with him. Daddy said in an interview he convinced his dad to move more into the central area of Tulsa because the west side was becoming such a tough environment for kids. Daddy attended and graduated from Tulsa Central High School, which was located at 7th and Cincinnati at the time. He got affiliated with the boxing club at the YMCA and boxed at a weight of 95 lbs when he was a senior in high school.

In the 1932 Tulsa Central yearbook, Paul Simmons is described as "A likable chap who possesses pluck and ambition and a fighting spirit." At their 50th class reunion, Daddy wrote a remembrance about a former English teacher, "Lulu Beckington laughing hysterically at some of my spelling, then hugging me to show she still loved me... I was later her milkman for a time..."

Just Call Me Pete

At some time during his high school years, he worked at Tulsa's first Warehouse Market at 8th Street and Boston. He was stock boy and customer service clerk, which consisted of stocking the shelves with products as well as carrying groceries from the checkout stand to the customers' cars. Even after all those years, in an interview he still remembered the names of all the people with whom he worked:

Originally known as the Colonial Store, C.V. Cox changed and re-organized the store renaming it Warehouse Market. It was the first supermarket in Tulsa. I was hired to stock and carry packages. There were several men by the same name as mine. Paul Cox was the owner, Paul Beaver, the floor walker, Paul Crain, produce manager, and Paul McAnally. We had no electronic intercom system like they do now so when they needed me to carry out groceries, they would call loudly "Paul". I would jump and run to the front of the store. I remembered that "inside deal" my brother Earl and I had when we traded names. So before the end of my first day, I said, 'Just call me Pete'. From that day forward, the name stuck. I worked there for about a year for the fabulous wages of $8.00 a week.

Postcard that Paul's mother Mollie sent to him in the mail for his Graduation Day.

Graduation

Tulsa Central has always been a large high school. Even then, there were over 1,000 students in the graduating class. The seating was limited but Paul acquired two tickets for his commencement ceremony. He invited his Aunt Pearl German and his Grandma Neighbors. Coralee German Green recalls that when Grandma Neighbors came to town and saw the apparent need for nourishment in Earl, she decided she was going to take him back home with her. Earl returned to Hugo, where he attended school until 1933.

James had a difficult time staying in school enough to complete each grade. As the oldest child, he may have felt responsible for the other children at times, and when times became seemingly unbearable, he would quit school and get a job. James talked the least about his life and the trials he faced, so his daughter Jo Ann Simmons Smith knew very little about where he lived and attended school, although she knew he did finish school while living with Aunt Jane and Uncle John Moore when they owned and operated a boarding house in Oklahoma City. Going through his records recently, we discovered together James not only graduated from Foster High School in 1933 but was his class president. Jo Ann shared she knew he pressed on because he saw the value of an education.

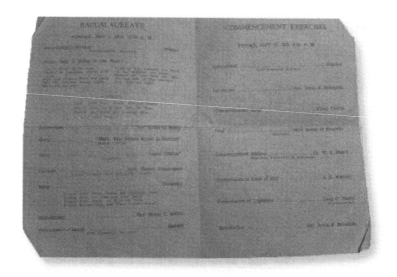

"James Simmons' graduation booklet 1933,
Foster High School, Oklahoma City, Oklahoma"

Daddy was always self-sufficient and was able to find jobs after graduation.

Then I found work candling eggs. I worked there for about a year. When I was 17 years old, I got a job on a farm. It was originally offered to someone else first. I'm always the second hand man. I was hired as a plowboy. I got up at 5:00 a.m., grabbed my milk bucket and headed toward the barn. I fed a team of horses, then milked 25 cows twice a day... ran to breakfast, had my second cup of coffee. They rang a "dinner bell", but if I didn't hear the bell I missed lunch. I got $17.00 for ½ a month plus board. I was between 17 and 18 years old and stayed about a year.

Family bonding together

During most of the 1930's, much of Oklahoma was referred to as the Dust Bowl. Those were difficult years for James and Paul as their dad Steve was trying to make ends meet. Around that time, Steve had an accident at a steel plant when a piece of steel flew into his eye and blinded him. That incident apparently caused him to lose his job or not able to work any more. It left Steve less hirable and able to support himself and the older boys except for some small farming.

After their high school years, James and Paul lived together with their dad share-cropping a sweet potato farm close to Beggs in about 1935. By that time James had married Dorothy Fields, whose parents owned a bakery in Broken Arrow. Daddy remembered their main diet consisted of day-old bread from the bakery and having to live on sweet potatoes every day for over a year. When families are usually enjoying sweet potato dishes during holidays like Thanksgiving, Daddy could not stand to eat sweet potatoes for many years when he and mother were first married.

When they lived together on the farm they took turns cooking what little food they had which was mostly bread and gravy.

They had a policy if anyone complained or criticized the food, that person would have to do the cooking the next day. So they were always cautious not to criticize. Daddy had a favorite story he always liked to tell:

> One time someone had made gravy and had salted it one too many times. When I took my first bite, I said 'Damn, that's salty...' (then hastily remembering the policy) and quickly added ... 'but just like I like it!'

Never Too Sick to Joke

Earl joined them after he graduated from high school. Earl remembered it was the first time he ever weighed over 100 lbs. They lived with or rented land from people by the name of Pugh. During that time, Daddy contracted malaria. As days passed, he grew worse. It did not look very hopeful he would recover. One of their neighbors who knew about natural remedies for health benefits told Earl to go pick a specific grass, perhaps horsetail, near the bank of the river. She told him to take it home and make some tea. He followed her instructions and helped his weak brother drink the tea, nursing him back to health. Daddy may or may not have known he was on his deathbed, but the Simmons children always seemed to have a strong quality of bonding together to help each other.

Earl remembered how serious that illness and event was. However, it did not deter Paul from joking and making light of the situation. It became another familiar family story and was always one of Earl's favorite stories to tell. He did not tell it because he was the hero who helped his brother live, it had another message. As he would tell the story, he could hardly tell it without emotion. He got to a poignant part about Daddy looking up and saying with a weak and frail voice, "Earl, if I die, then you'll be the best looking one in the family." When Earl would retell the story, he would just look at us and smile. He was waiting for a response to his punch line. This strong family survived by keeping their sense of humor. Daddy was no exception. He was especially known for his sense of humor throughout the years; it was a common factor among all the Simmons children as was seen frequently by all generations of the family from nieces, nephews to grandchildren, both young and old for the past 60 years.

The Wayne Jackson Family

Although Earl and Kathryn spent more time in their teenage years in Hugo, Oklahoma with Mollie's parents, Grandpa and Grandma Neighbors than the older two children, they lived in Broken Arrow again their last two years of high school. They lived with the Jackson family on the north side of 91st Street, also known as Washington Place in Broken Arrow across the street from the Peterson farm. The Jacksons had a 40 acre farm, which now is a park which bears the Jackson family name. Because the Jackson home was located north of 91st Street, it was in the Union School District. Both of the Simmons children worked for room and board while they lived there.

Being intelligent children, they were at the top of their class, as Valedictorian and Salutatorian. Records would show that because the year before Earl's senior year, he was ill with pneumonia and lived with the Neighbors in Hugo, resulted in Kathryn and him graduating in the same year. This was much to Earl's dismay. But more correctly, Union Public School did not offer the Agriculture class during Earl's junior year, so he had to wait and take Ag I and Ag IV both during his senior year. The competition was more personal to Earl because of those two issues.

However, Earl and Kathryn both had extremely strong math skills, which were very evident in their children in later years, as they nurtured those skills during high school and "homework" years. I was told even after a long day of work, Kathryn would come home and help her children around the kitchen table with their homework. Although they were a competitive family, Earl and Kathryn remained close kindred spirits for all the years of their lives.

Kathryn was also nursed back to health by Earl in much the same way as Paul was. Kathryn's daughters remember her saying several times during her lifetime, Earl saved her life. Years later, after the birth of Sandy, her fourth child, Kathryn became gravely ill. She lived in Kansas City and sent for Earl, who lived in Oklahoma. She felt he was the only one who could help her. He came and prayed for her and she immediately began to recover. Another time, when John was a baby, the older two girls LaVerne and Dorothy (Dottie) were about seven and eight years of age. Kathryn sent them to get crates to burn as firewood in the potbellied stove. It was near freezing temperatures in the place they were staying. Unannounced, Kathryn's brother Earl arrived at their door. When he saw their deplorable situation, he told them, "I'll be back." He left and later that day a large coal truck showed up and delivered coal to them. Earl came back later with a car load of groceries. LaVerne recalls their mother telling them if they didn't get any help, they were all going to die. She said Earl was like an angel to their mom. She believed he could do anything and trusted in his prayers.

"Look! No hands!" Pete shows off with a trick riding a tricycle.

Chapter 7
RIDIN' THE RAILS

Although the Simmons and Neighbors families continued to call him Paul or Paul Emmett, the rest of his friends just stuck with referring to him as "Pete". I may even interchangeably refer to him as Pete as much as Daddy. In an interview he gave several years later, he mentioned he "never really liked the name Paul anyway". It could be he felt the name Paul seems to be more formal as Pete appears to be more casual, friendly and approachable. Pete was definitely approachable to all who knew him.

During high school and after Pete had moved to Tulsa, he remained close to the Peterson. Ellen and Charles' youngest son Oscar was the same age as Pete. As first cousins, the two boys had a lot in common. After high school graduation, Pete had no certain future, because he could not afford to attend college as others. The stock market had crashed in 1929 and there were thousands of people without jobs and in soup lines for food. After graduation, Pete recalled:

> *Then I went to Mead, Oklahoma to plant oats for my aunt. My uncle Jim Moore (Jane's husband) had died. Mead is between Durant and Hugo. From there, I left for an East Texas oilfield in Kilgore. It was a brand new oilfield. I was the pro-ration man. Without knowing, I committed a felony. They were running "hot oil". They ran triangular wells: one good one, 1 pro-ration and 1 stinker. The boss said 'dig a ditch,' giving me no explanation, 'from this bad one to a good well and cover it over.' He was making a producer out of a dry well. When I realized it, I quit.*

Cast Your Bread Upon the Water

Roughnecks, a term describing the workers in the oil field, were a tough bunch of men who worked long and hard hours. When Daddy worked on the oil lease in Kilgore, Texas he was young man but hardly more than a boy. He recalled an impressionable story which was repeated to me several times through the years:

At the end of the day, these rugged tired men with leather-tough, dirty skin seemed to still have enough energy to gather in a circle to throw dice in a game of Craps. I watched intently and studied these individuals and the hard lives they endured. One man in particular made a remark one night that left an indelible impression on me. Although gambling was no doubt an undesirable trait to a respectable person of the day, this one roughneck gathered his winning pot of money together, stacking the denominations in order, facing the same direction but divided out a percentage of it. As I watched he said, 'This is the 10% that goes to the Lord. The rest I can spend on myself.' As he quoted a scripture from the Bible, he told me 'always remember to "Cast your bread upon the waters and after many days it will return". Son, if you give with good intention and give sincerely from your heart, the Lord will bring it back to you.'

As some may think of and refer to money given to a charity or church by this man as "blood money," Pete always looked at it differently from that point on. He decided never to judge the intent of a man's heart. Daddy taught me that one never knows what impression and influence another person may make on another.

After the "hot oil" incident Daddy came back home. His good friend and cousin, Oscar who was born only 13 days apart from him on the same farm, decided to strike out on their own adventures and hit the rails riding freight trains.

Some of Pete's stories may have sounded far-fetched, but after his death, I found a box of papers, postcards, small insignificant items—or it may have seemed. In that box were a few postcards written to his dad:

> *Oscar and I are in Durango and will hop a car tonight and be home in a couple of days.*

Pete especially liked to tell these railroad stories as he proudly admitted he was not just a "hobo" but considered himself a "bum". His railroad stories eventually became segways to make positive impressions on people.

This was a railroad story Pete enjoyed telling that he called a 'cheap trip':

> *Once we had been to Kansas City to visit my mom. I still could not get along with her. She always tried to tell me what I could not do. She had not had any control over my life in years. So we left. When we started to Denver, I had 75 cents in my pocket. We were going to catch the Rock Island Line. They always flew flags up front when they were carrying hot freight. They did not stop on green flags. But this time they had gray flags. I usually let Oscar catch the first car because he was slower than I was. He said he could not do it because it was going too fast. I said, 'Let me show you,' and as I grabbed the ladder, it slammed me up against the freight car. It was going too fast to get off, so I just rode along. I got hijacked for my 75 cents in Colorado Springs. I rode back to Amarillo, then to Oklahoma City. Not depending on anybody, I traveled the whole trip on 75 cents."*

Prison Is One Place I Know I Don't Want to Be

It was often common for Pete and Oscar to hop a train not knowing their destination, but just looking forward to the excitement of their next adventure. This was the case as they boarded a freight train one dark night leaving New Orleans, not knowing exactly which direction in Louisiana it was heading. They had settled in for the night in a corner of the box car with a small bunch of hay with very little comfort and warmth. Several hours and many miles later, the rocking of cars continued to lull the drifters in a half-asleep half-awake state. The darkest of night began to eventually welcome the early morning sun. Slowly and carefully sliding open the door of their boxcar to allow them a glimpse of their surroundings, the boys peered out the small opening. Much to their surprise, there were rows and rows of cabbage plants as far as the eye could see. Where could they be? They did not have much time to contemplate their situation and conjure up a plan as the steel wheels began to slow down then come to a screeching halt. The drifters were very familiar to this deafening sound and knew well to brace themselves for the sudden stop and prepare to crouch silently into a corner of the boxcar as to not be detected. Since there was no town or depot in view, they concluded it must be a random search to check the cars.

As the train inspector, known as 'the Bull,' pulled their car open wide, there was no way that they could conceal their cover. They were discovered and commanded to step down out of the car. As they climbed out of the boxcar, Pete and Oscar saw the railroad worker had a serious look of sternness, as he pointed a snub-nosed revolver at them. They surely could diffuse the situation with a little homespun humor as they had done many times before.

"Come on down out of there, boys!" the inspector shouted! After one small smart aleck quip by Pete, the inspector cocked his piece and pointed the revolver right at the end of Pete's nose. "Shut up if you want to live!" After some questioning, the shaking and frightened boys explained they had hopped the freight train late at night, not knowing its actual destination. From that point, the inspector realized their story made a little sense, an honest mistake and they were not intentionally at this location.

"Do you boys have any idea where you are?" he inquired. Because of their puzzled looks, he supplied the answer for them. "You're inside Louisiana State Penitentiary! And you need to climb right up into that boxcar and get yourselves outa here before you get yourself incarcerated!"

Pete admitted that was one of the most scared feelings he ever had in his entire life. Of course after the initial shock wore off, Pete saw a humorous side to the incident. It probably was his most very favorite story of all time to tell. He was able to use that experience often throughout the years as an object lesson to learn and an example of a "what not to do" situation and "places to avoid on one's life journey".

What is Different about this prison?

Louisiana State Penitentiary is located in Angola, Louisiana and is still considered as one of our country's most notorious maximum security prisons. Housing about 5,000 inmates, with a majority of them serving life sentences, this farm-like environment, a working agricultural complex, covers 18,000 acres of prime farm land.

What began as an insect-infested jail in New Orleans in 1835 became Louisiana State Penitentiary and moved to Baton Rouge. By 1844 it was leased to a private firm and used first by the Union

Army during the Civil War. It was then awarded to a Confederate Major, Major Samuel James, who eventually purchased an 8,000 plantation in Angola in 1880, which was named after the province in Africa from where former slaves came. After Major James' death, his family continued to control and occupy Louisiana's Correction system for 31 years. With reports of inmates being subjected to severe brutality over the years, the State of Louisiana resumed control of the facility and land.

Because the plantation was located in between 3 rivers, it was prone to and had seriously flooded 3 separate times: 1903, 1912 and 1922. By the third flood, people were ready to sell their land which enabled The Corrections' Board of Control to purchase the rest of the 10,000 acres bringing to total to 18,000 acres. During the depression years, it fell into disrepair so inmates were used to work on construction of the levee on the Mississippi River.

The land proved to still be fertile, so it has continued to be developed for traditional agriculture production and light industry utilizing cheap prison labor, being nicknamed "The Farm". So the endless rows of cabbage plants were only a small portion of the 18,000 acres. During that time following the days of the Great Depression, freight trains had access to deliver farm supplies and equipment onto the grounds of the Louisiana State Penitentiary and probably still do. That area of fertile land was no doubt an important part of feeding America during those days.

Today Angola Penitentiary is also home to 1,800 employees who live in town, described as the "Safest in America," located in the middle of the penitentiary. Also because it is no doubt well-guarded and also nicknamed the "Alcatraz of the South", most inmates perhaps do not challenge it. They were wiser than the two young boys from Oklahoma way back in an earlier time.

*Men standing in front of a boxcar was
a common sight in the 1930's.*

Frances Jenni Simmons, ca. 1940

Chapter 8
THE GIRL OF MY DREAMS

After a few years of "hoppin' freight trains, sowing wild oats and enjoying adventurous times, he and Oscar knew the time had come to settle down and return home. They had certainly gained a lot of experience the hard way and were ready to begin earning decent livings.

Tulsey-Town, Young and Carefree

The generation of 80 and 90-year olds at this writing, will remember the "Old Coliseum" in Tulsa, where young people enjoyed roller skating. There was another skating rink in Turley not as well known and called the Rainbow Room. Pete and his friend Leon Smock decided to go skating for entertainment one time. It was on one particular evening Pete met a petite but feisty young lady by the name of Frances Jenni. On more than one occasion, Frances told the story about how she would hide in the ladies' restroom, hoping to avoid him. She was a good skater, poised and graceful, but found Pete to not to be very agile on the skating floor. From his viewpoint, she was cute, small of stature. Because Pete was only slightly taller than about 5' 6", Frances was just his size, less than 5 feet tall.

Frances had been born and reared in Tulsa, graduating from Tulsa Central as well. It was not unusual during those years, for many families to have lived in poverty. Frances' family was no exception. She was the youngest child of eight, so most of her siblings were already grown and had left home. At her graduation commencement in 1936 she remembered wearing shoes with cardboard for soles. Her parents were (C.W.) Christian William "Chris" and Margaret Emily Reed Jenni. Grandpa Jenni was retired and the caretaker for the ballpark in Tulsa. Our mother recalled making donuts and selling them to earn money. She always taught us it is not a disgrace to be poor, but one can always be respected.

Growing up on a farm in Turley, Frances was not the only one in a poor family. She knew Ray Wilson, who later met and married Louise who later became a close friend. She recalled her family may have been poor, but Ray did not have any shoes at all and went to school barefooted. Other friends in Turley were Oleta and Arvena MacDonald. Arvena later became Frances' sister-in-law.

Remember Me?

Somehow, Pete won her over and began dating Frances. He liked calling her Fran, short and sweet like her frame. Once he settled down completely, Pete and Fran, they were married on September 1, 1940, when he was 26 and she was 21. The witnesses at their marriage were Tulsa and Turley friends, Harold Smock and Arvena MacDonald. Arvena later married James, Pete's brother. Their first wedding gift was a waffle iron given to them by Oscar Peterson.

Pete always reminded me that '*Remember Me*' was 'their' song. He often sang it for me as he reminisced those old Coliseum and Rainbow Room days in Turley. It was a popular song from 1937 sung by Bing Crosby. *Alfred Publishing Co., Inc. allowed me to reprint this special song.

*Newlyweds - 'Pete' and Frances Simmons
Their Marriage License*

Remember Me
Do you remember one September afternoon,
I stood with you and listened to a wedding tune,
And did not I go with you on your honeymoon?
Remember me?

Do you recall a cottage small upon a hill,
Where ev'ry day I had to pay another bill?
And if I'm not mistaken, dear, I pay them still,
Remember me?

I can see that little angel on your knee,
Can't you see, He kinda sorta looks like me,
For I'm the boy whose only joy is loving you,
Who worries till he hurries home when day is through,
And I'm the guy you give your goodnight kisses to,
Remember me?
Do you remember me?

• Used by permission: Alfred Publishing Co., Inc.

Pete and Fran made their first home in Tulsa, where he was working. Fran wasn't familiar with the background of the Simmons clan, nor the environment from which they came. She wasn't aware of their rearing and did not understand their sense of community being part of their security. Before long, Oscar and James moved into their apartment with them, if they were in between jobs and needed places to live. Granted this was just a little over ten years after the stock market crash and the rebuilding of our nation's economy.

But she did understand she was a newlywed and did not intend on sharing their nest with brothers and cousins. It was during a memorable genealogy trip back to Missouri in the early 1990's for just the two of us, she shared with me those stories of their early years. She told me she had to begin thinking of a strategy, because when she asked Pete to tell them to move, he probably did not have the heart to do it. At the time she was not employed, so she had the time during the day to read ads in the paper for places in Tulsa to rent. She recalled she would find a new place, go home and when Pete would come home from work, she would tell him privately, "We're moving. I found another place." She never said he objected, nor did she

Pete on the job in Tulsa, OK.

say they discussed the family arrangement. She was not very confrontational, so I can easily see she just made a plan and executed it. Then later, when one of the brothers or a cousin moved in again, she would just apartment hunt again. After awhile, everyone was employed so it wasn't a problem any more.

I believe she saw great potential in Pete's abilities, his uniqueness and especially perseverance, as seen at the roller skating rink. He no doubt appreciated the independence in her, but wanted to be the strong supportive force in her life. Whether or not he viewed Fran as fragile or vulnerable, he may have sensed she had a need for protection and love, which made a good husband and resulted in a good match.

During their early years of marriage, Pete had various jobs at Cain's Coffee Company and Meadow Gold Milk Company. He also worked some at the Tulsa Post Office, which proved later to be a good experiential move.

Santa Barbara, California

Our mom did love sunny California and living in Santa Barbara while my dad was in the Marines. They were stationed there in August of 1945 when they had their first child, a son. They had been married five years before Chris was

Pete and his Meadow Gold Truck after his route in 1940's

born. Many historical as well as personal events occurred that year. World War II ended and Pete's Grandpa Neighbors passed away that December.

Before our dad finished his tour of duty, he was stationed stateside. He had a part-time job in the evening.

*'Pete' Sailing and the
Santa Barbara Harbor, ca. 1945*

Always associating himself with famous people, he occasionally told us he worked as a dishwasher in Jimmy Cagney's Restaurant. But when we asked him if Mr. Cagney ever came into the restaurant, he admitted he had never met him because actors sometimes owned businesses they never operated.

Pete and Chris, "Pete and Re-pete"

It must have been fun for them to see movie stars and other famous people in many places they visited. Looking back in some of my old National Geographic and other magazines, many of us may remember the glamorous shots of Hollywood stars and cigarette ads. Mother and a friend were having coffee in a hotel restaurant one day, when a bellboy in a dapper uniform came through the lobby projecting his voice loudly, "Call for Philip Morris!" He paused and looked at the ladies and leaned forward, offering them each a cigarette, and asked, "Would you ladies like a Philip Morris?" I wonder

Santa Barbara Mission

if they had to stifle any giggles. One may imagine how many times they planted themselves in that hotel restaurant, knowing that one day they would coincidentally see him or others. It could have actually been an innocent first time. Of course, the older readers will remember that short little bellhop from TV commercials, saying that very phrase.

Those were the days.... the Greatest Generation, as they were called, made many sacrifices for their country for the sake of their families during the war. Things like gasoline and rubber tires were rationed as well as other items which were in a limited supply. They spoke of ration books for such things as shoes. I remember mother saying parents would spend their babies' shoe ration coupons sometimes. Since Chris was less than a year old and usually carried or strolled and did not wear out his baby shoes, they used his ration ticket for a new pair of shoes for our dad.

War and active duty brought separation. Most of the time, wives did not even know the location of their husband's assignment. Many letters our mother received from Pete were only stamped with "somewhere in the South Pacific".

During part of the time Pete was dispatched overseas, mother lived in Tulsa with her parents before Chris was born. She worked for a short time at Douglas Aircraft Corporation in Tulsa. I recall her telling me her job was to sort various sizes of nuts and bolts. It may have been tedious and boring, but she knew there was a more important purpose for her work.

By the time our dad was discharged from duty, he was back at work again in Tulsa. This time he was attending the University

A Marine and his girl.

of Tulsa and they had two children. Pete and Fran lived in a duplex close to TU that was owned by his Aunt Ellen Peterson Cannon. She owned a row of duplexes on 8th Street in Tulsa, so they rented one from her. As many wives did in those days, mother stayed at home. She enjoyed sewing for the family and now could sew for a girl. Although our mother attended school in Tulsa and had never lived anywhere else but Santa Barbara, she was willing to move to Broken Arrow to start a family. Daddy knew many of the hometown families, so Fran quickly fit in when they made the move.

Auxiliary Leader

Many of our friends were also in the military so Pete was involved in the American Legion as well as the Veterans of Foreign War. Naturally, she was in the both auxiliaries and hosted the ladies' meetings. I recall one meeting in our first house in Kenwood Hills at 71st and Main, I remember handing a little friend one of Daddy's business cards. It had credentials like: World War II Veteran on it. Although the girl was a year older than I was, when I showed it to her, she corrected me with "that's World War Eleven". Even at six or seven years old, my dad had engrained in my mind it was the second world war the United States had been involved in, and taught me about Roman numerals. That day, some of Pete's genes must have come out in me, because I remember feeling proud I knew something an older girl did not.

Not only was our mother a group leader for the American Legion Auxiliary and VFW Auxiliary, she was very sociable with church activities and was neighborly. Our neighborhood was new and just beginning.

Later when we moved to Haskell Addition, Mother continued to be active in school and community. As many mothers were, she was mostly involved in PTA. She especially was active when Haskell Elementary School was built and named.

Mother was always neighborly and friendly. I remember some of her favorite neighbors in Haskell Addition were Eudora Reed, a fourth grade school teacher, Mary Dobbins, Madge Jackson and Gerry Carpenter.

Other than working at Sears for a short time, Mother's only other job was at the Broken Arrow Tag Agency while we were still attending school. At first, Daddy was appointed the Tag Agent and she operated it, from about 1964 until 1967. Because of some poor management decisions in the main office in Tulsa, we were made sub-agents. Of course Daddy objected to being sub-agents to the Oklahoma Tax Commission and quit. Mother was appointed as the new Tag Agent, a sub-agent. There were several high school girls including Barbara and me who worked there after school and on Saturdays. There were quite a few ladies who worked there fulltime through the years. Her main "right hand man" was Loucille (Dobbins) Denison. Loucille was extremely efficient, friendly but professional. It makes me laugh at some of the fun times we had in our little office on El Paso next to the alley. It was located in the same building as Daddy's law office.

Later when my folks moved to Tahlequah Mother had an opportunity to attend college classes and eventually receive an Elementary Education Degree. That attainment in itself opened a brand new world to Mother. She not only enjoyed the academic accomplishment, but really enjoyed her years of being an elementary teacher.

Special Connection with My Mom

One of the most special times I had ever spent with my mother and had an opportunity and get acquainted with her as I had never done before, was on a brief genealogy trip to Missouri to visit her elderly cousins south of the St. Louis area. The year was 1992. Her cousins were Ruth and Alberta (Tommy) Hall who were unmarried daughters of Lucy Jenni Hall, her dad's sister. They lived in the Crystal City and Festus area, where they were born and lived their entire lives. The Jenni heritage began in and around Chur, Switzerland. Mother's great-grandfather came by ship to New Orleans and traveled up the Mississippi River to St. Louis. He settled in Festus and built a huge rock home he hauled in a wagon only a few at a time from a local rock quarry to the location where he lived his entire lifetime. Ruth and Tommy showed us the remains of that white rock house.

I suppose Mother's claim to fame was her connection to the lineage of Daniel Boone. Although she was not a direct descendant, she was more closely connected to the Phillips and Bryan families, from whom William Jennings Bryan came. While in Festus Mother and I listened intently while Ruth and Tommy reminisced about their mother's attendance at Bryan's funeral in 1925. Lucy was a young child at the time, but remembered quite a bit of detail and knew the rest of the Phillips and Bryan families quite well.

William Jennings Bryan was the prosecuting attorney in the famous "Monkey Trial" in which a school system was attempting to teach evolution. Bryan, a three-time candidate for United States President by the Democratic party won the case for his client. But the stress of the trial took a toll on his health. He died five days after the trial was completed.

Her Hero

Through over fifty-four years of marriage, Fran remained Pete's number one fan. She was always loyal to his many causes, supporting him and standing behind him every step of the way. She was a very special wife, friend and covenant partner to him then and for eternity.

Paul E. 'Pete' Simmons, a handsome Marine, ca. 1942

Chapter 9
THE FEW, THE PROUD, THE MARINES

The attack on Pearl Harbor on December 7, 1941, brought the United States into World War II. That "Day of Infamy," as President Franklin Roosevelt described the attack, brought an immediate expansion of America's military forces with many young men being drafted and others volunteering for the armed forces. As other able-bodied Americans did, James, Pete and Earl joined the service.

Pete had married Frances Jenni a little over a year before that day. After working at Cain's and Meadow Gold, he applied at the Tulsa Post Office. He passed the Civil Service test with flying colors and worked there as a postal clerk until he enlisted. The postal job proved to be a fortunate move because of his experience there.

James and Earl

James was in the United States Army, with the 106th Infantry Division called 'The Golden Lions' a name only used in WWII. James' company was surrounded in the early part of the Battle of the Bulge. He was wounded and captured and became a Prisoner of War in December, 1943.

James was imprisoned at Stalag IV for an undetermined time. Stalag IV was located in Pomerania, southeast of Belgard, Germany. As most P.O.W. camps were, conditions were deplorable and many suffered starvation. His daughter Jo Ann Simmons Smith has postcards James was able to send to his mother during the time he was incarcerated. The Russians liberated his camp at the end of the war.

James Simmons, POW in Stalag IV
was allowed to write Postcards to his mother

Earl shared with us about his military experience and said he was actually called up for the draft in February, 1941 at 24 years of age but was rejected because he only weighed 111 pounds. February, 1942, Earl married Virginia Yeckley. Shortly after that marriage, Earl applied again in the United States Army and this time was accepted and was stationed in Alaska, Arkansas, Oregon and Washington. His assignment in Alaska was Excursion Inlet for three months.

During that time, Virginia contracted tuberculosis and sought treatment in Arizona. That following September, 1942, Virginia died in Tucson. Officials in the American Red Cross had arranged for Earl to have a leave from military duty to be with her. She died the day after he arrived. He returned to Alaska and for three years was stationed at Cold Bay at the end of the peninsula. In early 1944, he was stationed in the Aleutian Islands for 20 months, until November, 1945. Earl was discharged from the Army in December 10, 1945 and in January, 1946, he returned to Bethany-Peniel College (now Southern Nazarene University) in

Bethany, Oklahoma, in January, 1946 at 29 years of age.

952nd Platoon U.S.M.C. San Diego, California
1942

Pete's Basic Training and Shipping Out

Pete entered the United States Marine Corps in 1942. He was always small of stature, but grew another four and a half inches while in the Marines. His mother, Mollie was not happy when Frances had to sign papers for Pete. She often said, "I don't know what I'll do without my brown-eyed boy." He was in the 952nd Platoon in San Diego, California, for basic training. Posted on the group photo is the following phrase: "U.S. Marines-- First to Fight".

Pete finished Basic Training and was an official "Leatherneck"

Up Anchor

New Caledonia, a collection of French-owned islands in the southwest Pacific Ocean, was considered the springboard in the Pacific during the years from 1942 to 1946 for more than one million troops as they were launched into the war zone. This island chain was the primary hub, providing the base for transportation from island to island in the conquest to regain control of that area.

"At the front" landing on the Island of New Caledonia

In November, 2014, I listened to an interview Pete made on a VHS video which was originally recorded on January 21, 1995. Pete described his experience with the United States Marine Corps in an interview with Mel Griffin, a Hospice representative about sixteen days before he passed away. He stated:

> *In 1942 we pulled up anchor in Port Loma, San Diego, California. It was thirteen days later that we dropped anchor at Noumea, the capital city of New Caledonia. I was flat on my back during that entire time.*

Pappy Boyington

Pete had always admired decorated World War II hero Major Gregory "Pappy" Boyington, a Marine Corps combat pilot with the legendary "Flying Tigers," the First American Volunteer Group that fought in the Republic of China Air Force in

Burma in 1941-42. Boyington had resigned from the Marines to fly with the "Flying Tigers." He became an ace, one who has shot down five enemy aircraft.

Pete discussed Chiang Kai-shek, the Chinese political and military leader of the Republic of China, and told how the Chinese got into the war with the Japanese. When the United States finally took Boyington back into the Marine Corps, he again became a flying ace. He later was awarded the Medal of Honor and the U.S. Navy Cross in recognition of his heroic action.

Pete described his encounter with Boyington in these words:

The first time I met Pappy it made quite an impression on me. I had a propensity for upset stomach, motion sickness, causing nausea. When the whistle blew 'all hands on deck—fire drill-- Clean Sweep – fore and aft', I laid in my sack, cause I was seasick. Chief Petty Officer came through and said, 'Mack, you'd better get on deck. You'll wind up in the brig.' I said to the Chief, 'They have a sack down there don't they?

Pretty soon this young Captain came through and said, 'Sea sick?'

'Yes Sir,' I replied. It was Pappy. He said 'I get the same way and I've been across this ocean six times.' Later I found out who he was. I kept up with him during the war and afterwards. Pappy was in Fighter Squadron 214, under General Roy S. Geiger.

Later Pappy was shot down in the middle of the night—was in his "Mae West" when a Jap sub came up and took him prisoner. When Pappy wrote his book of memoirs and was making his tour after the war, I got a personally autographed copy from him. I reminded him of the conversation that I had with him. It was always very special to me.

In The Jungle

When we arrived in Noumea, New Caledonia, I was on work detail, loading supplies and was then transferred to the Henry T. Allen, just a little bucket. (The USS Henry T. Allen, APA-15, was a Harris-class attack transport ship that served with the U.S. Navy during World War II. The ship operated between New Guinea and Australian ports, carrying both American and Australian troops in support of the Allied offensive in New Guinea and the Solomon Islands.)

Pete making light of the WARNING: UNSAFE Drinking water

I started out in Es Spirito Santo in the New Hebrides Islands. Since there was no fighting there, we began breaking ground, building tents for Headquarter squadron first rank. There had been no civilian troops there before us, so when we landed we were told: 'You may NOT...... under any circumstances associate, affiliate or visit with the savages on this island.' The savages there were head hunters. Associating with the cannibals in these camps was strictly off limits. Missionaries had been there. I had enough Latin to know that Es Spirito Santo meant "Holy Spirit" apparently named by the previous visitors to the island.

My greatest trophy of the war was a picture of head

Missionaries had come to this Island and named it
"Es Spirito Santo" - The Holy Spirit

hunters holding two heads in their hands still dripping.... I don't know what happened to that picture, it was a prized possession. I do have one picture that, of course was taken and was strictly off limits, with a Sergeant Major in it (showing the picture on the video) and with "a flunky on the right". (He did not identify either person.)

The Marine Unit paid the natives 17¢ per day to keep the area clean.

One of Pete's favorite photos:
Forbidden to associate with Headhunters

We had a good relationship with the island people. We paid them 17¢ per day to pick up coconuts and keep the camp neat. We paid them in copper because that was durable. I was there several months. It rained 15 inches every year.

Experience Trumps Chance

Over the course of Pete's Marine Corps tour, he served with units on several islands in the South West Pacific war theatre. Throughout my years growing up, he occasionally mentioned the names of the islands where he was stationed, but he never spoke of a timeline, or of his specific duties. I didn't understand the magnitude of the war time duty during our conversations until the writing of this book.

Pete simply described that service with these words:

I was in the Marines as a Buck Private, with no stripes. I came out as a Master Sergeant with 6 stripes. I was always winding up in a place of critical need, and consequently was promoted. Every time they came around, I got one.

While I was there, the Colonel discovered reading my record books—that I had been a postal clerk—the mail was piled high as this room (pointing). I learned "only volunteer one time", from then on I learned only follow orders when called on. I was immediately promoted to Corporal. Then Captain Staver flew me to Guadalcanal to straighten their mail up. He told me, 'Simmons, your time is up, time for you to go home, but you only have 5 stripes. I'm not going

Mother was relieved to hear Pete was safe and Coming Home! Pete was welcomed back at the Tulsa Post Office when he was on leave.

to send you back yet. Don't ask why. I'm gonna send you back after I give you your 6th stripe.' Other troops were coming in, who were more qualified than I was and he didn't want me to leave there without out promoting me first. He appreciated the work that I had done. So after I received my 6th stripe, he sent me home.

During the videotaped interview, Pete spoke of his weapons collection display and discussed a Japanese sniper rifle, with a sling on the side. He also held for viewing the Garand M-130-caliber rifle which was the standard weapon for the Marines, and then demonstrated how to insert a bullet in the chamber of the rifle.

Pete taking a break from his daily duties - Stateside

Draped over the couch beside Pete for the interview were two uniforms worn by him during his World War II service— the Marine green duty uniform and the beautiful Marine dress blues, the most recognizable uniform of the Marine Corps.

He was buried in his dress blue uniform.

Semper Fi

In 1988 I drove Mother and Daddy to Oklahoma City for a cousin's funeral. The memorial was for Alva Earl German. Besides an older sister Cora Lee German Green, Aunt Pearl Neighbors German had twin sons, Elba Pearl and Alva Earl. Daddy nicknamed them Bunting and Bill. Elba and Earl were born in Hugo and lived in Central Oklahoma, around Seminole. I was acquainted with Elba who had daughters close to my age.

From the pastor I learned Earl was retired but loved to drive a school bus for an area school. His death was unexpected, and students were shocked when they heard about Earl's heart attack. When we experience the death of a friend or loved one, we regret not having one last conversation. We were extended an invitation to write a note to Earl and place the note inside the casket as we passed by. I felt this was an excellent object lesson for students and other friends to express their thoughts and feelings to have closure.

I shared with my dad what I had written in my note to Earl. I wish I had gotten to know Earl but did not have that opportunity. When I asked Daddy what he wrote, he simply said, "Semper Fi!" obviously because his cousin Earl was a fellow Marine and shared a special bond of camaraderie. He explained Semper Fidelis is Latin for "Always Faithful" or Always Loyal (to the brotherhood). He reminded me there is no such thing as an "Ex-Marine." Once a Marine, always a Marine!

From a World War II veteran to my genealogist friend, John Rush, USMC, who has served in battle more recently, they understand and interpret their motto and mission the same.

The term Semper Fi or Semper Fidelis, our motto translates to Always Faithful. To my fellow Marines and me both past and future it is so much more. It is a way of life; you know that the Marine to your left or right will die to protect you just like you would them. Unlike other branches of the service we earn our title Marine. It is not given. Whether you are an officer or enlisted we must start our careers on the yellow footprints of San Diego, CA; Parris Island, SC or Quantico, VA. From the songs we sing while running and marching to the overall his-

tory of the Marine Corps we are taught the importance of Semper Fi.

Master Sergeant Paul E. 'Pete' and Frances Simmons
1945

Semper Fidelis became the Marine Corps motto in 1883. It

guides Marines to remain faithful to the mission at hand, to each other, to the Corps and to country—no matter what. The motto distinguishes the Marine Corps bond from any other. It goes beyond teamwork—it is a brotherhood that can always be counted on. Daddy considered it to be the largest fraternity of brotherhood in the world

Becoming a Marine is a transformation that cannot be undone, and Semper Fidelis is a permanent reminder of that. Once made, a Marine will forever live by the ethics and values of the Corps.

The Marines could have just stated their motto in English but by translating Always Faithful into Latin, it lends sophistication and credibility. Marines are not "Usually" Faithful, not "Sometimes" Faithful…. but ALWAYS FAITHFUL.

*Paul E. Simmons, young, inexperienced,
but eager to learn*

Chapter 10
PREACHER OR LAWYER

As Pete was departing from active duty with the Marines after World War II in Santa Barbara, California, his commanding officer exhorted his marines to go back to their hometowns, re-enter civilian life and give back to society. He encouraged them to make a difference, to put the past of the war behind them and look for ways to serve their communities. That made quite an impression on this young marine and father. He already had a sense of service. Those four Simmons siblings already had the gumption to be survivors of a hard life because they had often experienced helping each other.

He perhaps mulled over in his mind the options that were set before him. He probably had already dismissed the thought of being a preacher. It was obvious to him he should take advantage of attending college on the GI Bill, an option he would not have had before the war. So Pete embarked upon a new career—or at least a new adventure. Pete enrolled at The University of Tulsa in 1946 and was joined by his long-time friend, Randall West. A year later Pete's second child, and first daughter was born the summer before classes began for the fall semester. I was that child, Janice Ellen Simmons. Our family lived at 923 S. Darlington in Tulsa, across the street from Frances' sister and brother-in-law, Howard and Bess Angel, other long-time Tulsans.

At that time students did not have to declare majors, but both eventually became lawyers. Pete said this in an interview:

"I never had any desire to be a lawyer, did not person-ally know anyone who was a lawyer, and did not even

know what a lawyer did, I just knew I needed a basic education. My folks were divorced so I had no means of paying for college."

*Pete and Fran made their home at
923 S. Darlington, Tulsa, OK during law school*

Pete and West attended Spanish class from 7:30 to 8:30 a.m. then went to the coffee shop to practice their new language. The next hour, they had French class. They somehow muddled through both classes and learned the two languages by interjecting a French word into a Spanish sentence if they could not think of the Spanish word that fit. Although highly unorthodox, this practical method of conversing came in handy at a later time in his life.

Another friend Pete met at The University of Tulsa was Elliot Howe. Howe attended night school. Pete and Howe graduated from law school and began practicing their profession the same year. They stayed connected all the years they were lawyers, seeing each other in court occasionally. Howe eventually became a minute clerk, and later moved into the County Commissioner's Office. Howe's daughter, Sally Howe Smith, presently our Tulsa County Court Clerk, recalled when she graduated from high school she met Pete. She worked for the court clerk and recalled Daddy coming into their office. On numerous occasions she saw Daddy put his hand flat on the counter and jump, landing flat-footed on the other side. An agile feat to achieve; a great story to share.

I Don't Want My Son to be a Liar

The young couple and new family were content with the excitement of education and financial stability right around the corner. But not everyone was happy about the situation. Pete's mother, Mollie told him she did not like the idea of him being a lawyer. She told her son, "I don't want my son to be a lawyer. Lawyers become liars. I don't want my son to become a liar." Although Mollie was never satisfied with Pete's decision, that did not deter him from his new goal and future plans.

Growing up I somehow was aware of underlying feelings of dissention between my dad and his mother. None of us truly knew the whole story behind his feelings of anger and sadness.

Not Just Anyone Can Be a Teacher

During the time of Pete's college career, he carried a full load of classes while working fulltime at different jobs. His freshman year, Pete was allowed to enroll in many of his major classes. In 1946 the college allowed students to attain their major degree while completing their Bachelor degree. He always believed learning the subject he was studying was more important than the grade he attained.

Pete always spoke his mind, not just sometimes... always. One of Pete's college courses not only challenged him but his classmates. He completed the course with a "D." Pete approached the professor to negotiate a better grade. We might presume the professor told Pete he should have applied himself more and tried a little harder for a better grade. Pete already had learned to plead his case, and therefore analyzed the situation.

Because several other classmates either made a "D" also or received a failing grade, Pete knew he had nothing else to lose. He knew he had no chance of having his grade changed, so he just laid all his cards on the table. With no surprise to anyone who knows Pete well, his conclusion and rebuttal was "since the majority of this class either failed the course or received a below average grade, it must be a direct reflection of your ability to teach the subject."

The Most Important Course in Pete's College Career

Years later, Pete had many opportunities to visit schools or civic organizations, to speak at special occasions such as Law Day, Veteran's Day, and other patriotic events. He always enjoyed asking people his favorite question if they inquired about attending law school. He especially liked asking it to young students: "What do you think is the most important course to take if you were attending law school?"

He had various responses such as debate, history, civics, or just law

Pete's law school picture at University of Tulsa, 1949

class in general. He would have a broad grin across his face as he would proudly announce that "English grammar" is the correct answer. Then he would proceed to explain one has to spend several hours writing out reports, scripts and legal documents which need to be grammatically correct as well as legally correct. Preparation for the courtroom is far more time-consuming than being in the courtroom itself. Pete was a real stickler for using proper grammar in his presence and noticed it if one did not. First impressions are the most important and lasting ones. He believed that one does not get a second chance at a first impression.

Not all the Lights have to be Green

As Pete continued his interview:

When I came back from the war, I went back to the Post Office and worked as a postal clerk in Tulsa. I had a 5 point preference because of my military experience. Because I still considered a college education to be important and could take advantage of the G.I. Bill, I quit my job and started college. I enrolled at the University of Tulsa in 1946 and I graduated in May, 1950. I drove a taxi at night the first year that I practiced law. While most new attorneys delayed setting up their practice to build up their business, not I. Not all the lights have to be green for me to begin a new venture in business.

Power of Persuasion

As Pete leaned more toward a career in law, he knew he had verbal gifts and a knack for the power of persuasion. Later, when speaking at schools, students would tell him they

After a full day's work Pete was exhausted. He had two speeds; full-throttle or collapsed.

would make good lawyers because they like to argue. Pete would tell them there was much more to being a lawyer than arguing. Being a lawyer required diplomacy, patience, listening, communicating and most of all strategy. Whoever has the best strategy is often the winner in a legal matter.

Roads and Pathways

Daddy had such a love for poetry, he remembered verses from complete poems he learned and recited when he was in elementary and high school. He often quoted some of the more familiar phrases from Shakespeare.

Many times I heard Daddy use the words "opportunity" and "security" when making comparison with choosing professions or life-long jobs. When he was young he had several different jobs and depended on someone else to be his boss. But as he got older, he liked being his own boss, especially with his choleric personality. Security represented to him a person who worked for someone else. It could be working an eight hour job and going home with no further responsibility. He compared drawing a weekly paycheck to always being dependent on someone for a paycheck. Daddy always continued to learn and grow intellectually because he sought opportunity. Contrary to what was the right way to believe, everyone makes their life choices based on different criteria. I believe because the people he depended on when he was young disappointed him, he learned to not depend on anyone.

One of his favorite poems was The Road Not Taken by Robert Frost. It actually describes a lot about Pete's life. The road traveled a lot was smooth and worn down and made a trip more passable unlike the road covered with fallen trees and overgrown brush. One was easier and the other more difficult. Pete always took the more difficult route but to him it was rewarding. As both Frost and Pete recognized, taking another path or direction can truly make a difference on one's life.

Preachers and lawyers have something in common in their professions. They both interact with people who often are at crossroads in their lives or who must make decisions or changes. They both must make a plea for mercy on behalf of the person and have the power to persuade. These two professions are actually a great deal similar. So, Pete made the choice. A lawyer it is!

Pete examining an abstract in his law office;
he referred often to the law books given to him by
Judge Frederic Righter.

Chapter 11
BACK TO BROKEN ARROW

Once Pete graduated from law school at the University of Tulsa, he was ready to take on the world. One case at a time. Deciding to return to his hometown, he hung his shingle at 1001 N. Main, Broken Arrow in 1949. I first saw that address in print from an article in the Broken Arrow Ledger. Much to my surprise Pete's first office was in his home—our home. My friend and newspaper reporter, Roberta Parker, gave that article to me. Mrs. Parker subsequently gave me several articles in which Daddy appeared and was very encouraging in keeping Daddy's memory alive as part of Broken Arrow history and city government. She, as well as others, encouraged me to write about Daddy.

Pete and Frances bought their new home in the brand new housing addition called Kenwood Hills, nestled at Kenosha and Main. Pete, being a visionary and entrepreneur in his own right, obviously saw the advantage of locating at this spot. He saw the potential and value of being a homeowner instead of renting a home. It was a sign of belonging and one of permanence. Built in 1945, our home was one of the first houses in Kenwood Hills. I remember other homes being built during the time we lived there until I finished the fourth grade, from 1949 until the summer of 1957.

Some of our former friends from Kenwood Hills were able to attend the reception we held to celebrate what would have been Daddy's 100th birthday last November 14, 2014. Several of the conversations our friends contributed that day helped to reconstruct our memories of our precious little neighborhood where everyone knew each other. Barbara Harper was in attendance along with Butch Mays. Hoil and Mahala Thompson were the most helpful.

Some of our first neighbors were John and Ruth Tadlock and their daughter, Renee. Ruth was the sister of Hoil Thompson. John worked for Broken Arrow Schools in the Industrial Arts department. He and the shop students built at least two of the homes in Kenwood Hills. Mahala shared with me that Jay Metzger and Ronald Corp are two that she remembers being in high school during that time. John and his class built the house behind ours which the Tadlocks lived in and the one across the street from ours, where Joe Vaughn's family lived. My folks became very good friends with Hoil and Mahala through the Tadlocks.

In the summertime, I remember waking up to hammering of lumber as Broken Arrow, "Tulsa's bedroom community," grew quickly. According to Life Magazine, Broken Arrow was one of the fastest growing towns in America. Part of Broken Arrow's growth could have been attributed to American Airlines employees being transferred to the Tulsa plant from New York. Our neighbors, the Regenhards, were one of those families. They bought the Tadlock's house. Another American Airlines family, Carolyn and Richard Hall lived across the street. We enjoyed the model trains he built.

Perry and Barbara (Waggoner) Harper were neighbors just to the north of us. Barbara was a sweet young mom, having one of their two children Terry Lynn born while living there. The Harpers later moved and became co-owners of Mac Trucks in Tulsa when Rick was born. We were well-acquainted with both Perry's and Barbara's families, Mrs. Harper and John and Edith Waggoner. Perry's mother lived on 71st Street not too far from us. Later Perry and Barbara sold their house to her parents, John and Edith Waggoner. We also were friends with

Maxine Harper Kindley and her husband Carmine. It wasn't until years later I realized that Maxine was Perry's sister. I had never known her by her maiden name.

Kenwood Hills was a nice neighborhood with good neighbors. Some of our other neighbors were Buck, Doris and Carolyn Wallace, who owned and operated Food Palace, Ralph Blane, Emma Jo and George Hunsecker, Lawrence and Lucille Brewer, Butch Mays, Jack, Ann and Rodney Murray, the Jones,' the Sweets' and their families. Our neighbor Jenny Mae Lidtke was also my Home Economics teacher later in high school. That was the old part of the neighborhood before the remainder of the addition was built going further up the hill.

Pete and Frances had fond memories of their first house and their neighbors in Broken Arrow. I remember vividly living in the little white house in Kenwood. Some of the neighbors above were also clients of my dad through the years.

An Heirloom

Although I was too young to remember Daddy's office ever being in our home, at some point, the address was changed to 1001 Highland Drive. He moved his office to 115 S. Main within the next year before he became the city judge in 1951.

His new law office may have appeared meager, but Pete was proud to decorate it with a collection of law books displayed in handsome wooden bookcases given to him by Judge Frederic Righter. The judge had been a longtime Broken Arrow resident and respected judge before he retired. I knew Judge Righter only through that story. Daddy cherished Judge Righter's gift, his prized possession and displayed the books for as long as he practiced law.

Pete's First Client

Toward the end of his career in one of our conversations, Daddy told me about his first office in our home on Highland Drive. I do remember living in the back of that first office at 115 S. Main. Because I was so young, I always assumed that we lived in the office while our new house was being built. I was between five and six years old. Daddy explained that he did have an uphill struggle starting a legal career in Broken Arrow, but he persevered. After all, Broken Arrow already had one lawyer and was still a small town. At one time Daddy probably had a difficult time admitting he had suffered a bad financial year in business. He told me he moved his family to the back of the office and rented their sweet little home in order not to lose it to foreclosure.

One of Pete's first clients, if not the very first client, was a lady who needed to have a will. She asked him how much it would be and he gave her a price of $5.00. As I recall him telling me, she decided to think it over and come back another time. He saw her in town and asked her about her will. Her response was when she visited another lawyer in town and told him Mr. Simmons had quoted her a price of $5.00, the other lawyer told her he would draft a will for her for only $4.00. So she decided to accept the lower price from the other lawyer. As a struggling attorney, Pete needed her business.

The economy was still recovering from World War II, and most people had lived through the depression learning to be frugal with their money. That one act, that one decision of a client, made a lasting impression on Pete. He had a difficult time not taking things personally. That may have been a major factor, if not THE major factor that affected his entire legal career and was a turning point in his attitude. To the client it may have been only a money factor, but to Pete it was a loyalty and relationship factor. He was especially disappointed at the other lawyer whose business was more well-established. He felt he lost her business because he was undercut by $1.00. He was often heard saying, "When life hands you lemons, you can choose to make lemonade." From that point on, Pete was determined he would always help new lawyers coming into town. He did just that.

Lawyer or Antique Dealer

Pete was not a shrewd businessman. His mission was always to help people whether they could pay their bill or not. He was no doubt familiar with rejection as well. I believe he must have had a firm philosophy in his business; never turn anyone down, even if they could not pay for the services. If they could not pay cash, they offered barter. Bartering was more common in the 1950's than now.

Among some items I recall that Pete accepted for payment of services were: an old cane-seated wheelchair (perhaps like the one Old Man Potter used in the movie "It's a Wonderful Life"), a pump organ and a Victrola. Those were probably antiques even then, and would possibly be coveted by vintage and antique dealers in today's times. However, at the time, they were useless to us. He may have accepted anything of monetary value because he was more concerned about helping to preserve the client's dignity and worth.

When I was attending the grand opening of the new Broken Arrow Historical Museum in 2005 I saw an antique radio on display that once was owned by Daddy. I wasn't aware of its history until then. The information on the display card read:

Atwater Kent Radio on display at Broken Arrow Historical Museum
· Courtesy of Broken Arrow Historical Museum, Broken Arrow, Oklahoma

Atwater Kent Radio
Model 20 Mfg 1924
This may be the oldest radio in Broken Arrow
This Atwater radio was given to me in 1960
By Pete Simmons, a lawyer and judge in Broken Arrow.
We were in Scouts together and since I collected old radios he let me have it.
I changed some tubes. It was a 5 tube set, repaired some circuits and got it going again just like new. Our old timer Howard Fisher says that on Main Street was Raymond Goodner Electric Company and Appliance Store that sold the Atwater Kent. That was in 1924.
The radio cost
About $100.00, batteries and speaker extra.

A gift to the BA Museum by
Andy and Doris Anderson, May 2009

Give and It Shall Be Given to You

Many other former friends and associates also came to Daddy's birthday reception that we held in November of 2014. Peggy Sherrell Van Dyke saw an array of pictures and memorabilia on display at the Broken Arrow Historical Museum. Peggy told me a story about working for Daddy when she was in high school. A client came in to pay on his account for Pete's services rendered from an earlier occasion. He paid a substantial amount and after he left the office, Daddy turned to Peggy and said, "The Lord always provides. I did not have the money to make my house payment until this very moment." That statement and testimony made such a lasting impression on Peggy, she remembered it sixty years later.

Be Specific

Another favorite story worthy to mention is the one about a widow who came to seek out Pete's legal services. After discussing her situation, doing the paperwork and finalizing the legal preparations and conversation, she asked him, "How much do I owe you?" Now often, especially in later years, he did not charge an hourly fee or any fee at all. But he was building his business during the early days, so he simply replied, "Twenty-five." Opening her little coin purse, the humble widow retrieved a quarter and laid it on the desk. He thanked her and never said anything else to correct her.

Municipal Judge

Pete was gentle on widows and orphans but tough on the establishment. I do not know if other civil servants realized at first exactly how tough he could be in the public arena, but with time they certainly discovered his "spirit and pluck". Within his first year after graduating from law school, he was appointed Broken Arrow's Municipal Judge. An article appeared in the Broken Arrow Ledger only twelve days after our new baby sister, Barbara Lisbeth arrived, completing our family of five.

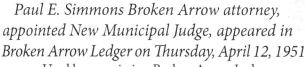

Paul E. Simmons Broken Arrow attorney, appointed New Municipal Judge, appeared in Broken Arrow Ledger on Thursday, April 12, 1951
• Used by permission Broken Arrow Ledger

Paul Simmons New Municipal Judge
Thursday, April 12, 1951

Attorney Paul E. Simmons has been appointed Municipal Judge, replacing Judge B.F. Mullins who recently resigned. The appointment was made by acting mayor Alvin Eskridge and approved by the city council.

Simmons, a combat Marine veteran of World War II, received his law degree at the University of Tulsa and was admitted to the bar in September of 1950.

He served as commander of the local Billy Robertson post, VFW last year and maintains his law office at 115 South Main.

A Cornucopia of Plenty

Not only were large vintage items bestowed upon Pete for his services, but also perishables. Throughout the years, we also had a bounty of food given to us, sometimes by the bushel basket, especially in the summer and fall growing seasons. Pete was willing to accept whatever his clients had available and wanted to give. I never once heard him say, "No, I only accept cash or check." I often heard, "Just pay when you can." However, most of the time, these words were spoken: "You don't owe me anything. Just go out and help someone else who needs it."

Daddy's longtime friend and fellow veteran, Jim King, told me more than once, "Your dad should have died a millionaire if he had not given everything away." Daddy's goal was not one of monetary value, but to truly give to others. I believe Mr. King knew that, but did not like to see Pete go without in order to meet others' needs.

I was with Daddy once when he took his new 1963 Ford pickup truck and delivered it to someone else's driveway. He had Mother to pick him up to drive him home. He did not tell me ahead of time where his destination was.

That, my friends, is an uncommon heritage which can be taught but often is not. In that way, he led by example. I have yet to see those actions exhibited by anyone else to that level. There is no other way to explain it. It surely is a God-given gift, one to the extent of which he would abandon his own wants to meet the needs of others. Pete would literally give the "shirt off his back" if necessary. That gift lives on and has been passed on to his direct descendants. I've also seen that gift exhibited by and to the descendents of Pete's siblings, who may have felt abandoned at one time.

Pete had finally made his way back to Broken Arrow in

hopes he could give back to his community and make a difference in the lives of people. Coming to Broken Arrow promised new beginnings for young families and for Pete Simmons and his family. Home Sweet Home.

'Gallopin Pete' made his mark on Broken Arrow from the 50's.

Chapter 12
MAIN STREET BUSINESSES

Broken Arrow's Main Street was lively during the 1950s. Broadway was the dividing line between North Main and South Main. Other than Daddy's office in our home, his first law office was located at 115 S. Main. The First National Bank now occupies the entire block from Broadway to Commercial. Many people have fond memories of that block on Main Street, from the Food Palace on the north end and First National Bank on the south end, with several different establishments in the middle. The Old Crystal Theatre had run its course from the 1940s through the early 1950s, and was replaced by Buddy Dill's dad's furniture store. Next was Pete's office, then Al's Café to the south. Stevenson's garage was in between the bank and the café. Imagine approaching the driveway of the garage business with caution just in case a driver was pulling out of the garage in his recently repaired car. I remember the sign at the entrance/exit: "Honk when exiting."

Gallopin' Pete

As business grew, Pete found himself going to the bank often. But his gait was not typical. He was seen and often remembered "running" to the bank in his typical unique style. Yes, he was always in a hurry…. never being unproductive for one moment. But for Pete, it was an everyday occurrence to run, not walk to the bank. I'm sure people noticed but perhaps never knew running in a sprint had become a habit of his mentioned earlier as a young man working on Bob Smittle's farm. Perhaps Pete's desire to hurry and complete chores is the reason he began running the horses to the spring.

Always on the Run

Pete not only was seen running up the street to the bank but always was on the run getting to court in Tulsa. A few years ago Arlis Wilson shared a story with me. He and his brother Onis ran a gas station on the corner of Main and 71st Street (Kenosha). Daddy stopped in to fill up his tank with gas. He accidentally ripped the pocket on his suit coat getting out of the car. He went inside the building and asked Arlis if he had a stapler. Arlis handed him one and Pete quickly stapled the inside of his suit and went on his way. Arlis really enjoyed Pete's resourceful creativity.

Waving Old Glory

Downtown businesses in Broken Arrow flew the American flag in front of their offices or stores on particular patriotic holidays. As I recall, the Jaycees (Junior Chamber of Commerce) rented flags to the businesses as one of their fundraisers. As a former Marine Pete was very patriotic and felt like it was a privilege to display our American flag, but also believed it was an honorable decision to own one's own flag to fly. He was proud he had fought under the 48-star flag. He said it was a matter of principle as it usually was with Pete, he did not participate in the yearly fundraiser. He always flew his own flag, even if it was his 48-star flag long after we had admitted 50 states into the union. There may be a few older businessmen who may remember how Pete maintained his stand on this issue.

Broken Arrow Fire Department volunteers check the hoses on their truck. In the background, one can see Tucker's Barber Shop and Beauty Shop, Naifeh's Grocery Store. Nill's Grocery and market and Barnsdall Gas Station.
• Courtesy of Broken Arrow Historical Museum, Broken Arrow, Oklahoma

Volunteer Fire Department

A very common occurrence on Main Street and side streets was the flurry of activity that commenced whenever the fire alarm was sounded. Our dedicated volunteer fire department came running from all directions. Pete always spoke highly of the people who unselfishly protected our community. He admired their service to our hometown.

Jennings Jewelry was right directly across from Daddy's office; it seemed as if Chester Jennings was the first out the door of his business, like a rodeo bull out of the chute. Jimmy Kemp ran down the street from his hardware store. Howard Fisher ran up the street from Dickason Goodman and others from all directions.

None of these men were paid or compensated for their work, hence the words volunteer firemen. Howard Fisher was later part of Broken Arrow's Fire Department as a paid employee, eventually becoming Fire Chief. Much can be said about Howard Fisher's contribution to Broken Arrow. Without him, our community would not have a historical museum, or at least one with the quality it has today. Much to his wife Thelma's chagrin, he saved every antique and piece of Broken Arrow history large and small in his home, garage and his mother-in-law's garage as well as vacant business buildings and property in the downtown area when it was not being rented or used.

Pete probably would have been involved in volunteering for the fire department too, had his schedule allowed it. Sometimes his time was not his own and depended upon his court appearances, which was very demanding of his time.

Coffee Break

By this time Broken Arrow had many cafés, restaurants and eating establishments to allow for an occasional break from work and have coffee with friends, business associates and protégés. Crawford's, Woody's and other hamburger cafés were available, but the upscale businessmen stopped their work in order to gather occasionally at Lindy's, which was in the middle of the block on the east side of the street between Commercial and Dallas. One could imagine the intelligent philosophical opinions oozing from the mouths of Broken Arrow's finest leaders and successful businessmen.

Among those was Howard Fisher, who began his adult work career with Dickason Goodman Lumber Company in the position of collecting debts from past due accounts. Howard recalled as soon as he would walk into Lindy's, Pete would say to him, "Isn't that right, Howard?" Attempting to draw him and get a pre-committed statement into this conversation. Of course Pete full well knew his controversial statements did not have agreement.

"Pete, if anyone is for something, you're against it, and if anyone is against something you are for it!" Then they would all have a good laugh! No one wanted to be on the side of the nonconformist, but Pete did not mind standing alone. He was neither afraid to speak his mind nor give his opinion. He always appreciated Howard's friendship through the years.

Editorials are His Specialty
"Paul Revere Rides Again"

There were actually people who agreed with statements and opinions Pete occasionally made publicly. He was disappointed they would not speak up and often was found standing alone in the ring. At least once he paid for space in the Broken Arrow Ledger, on Thursday, April 12, 1956 when his "editorial" appeared in a regular news section instead of the editorial page.

His subject was the Postmastership in Broken Arrow. Pete said he believed "75% of the people in Broken Arrow are really independent in their thinking and voting but are registered in one or other large political parties."

Dear Editor:
The response to my previous efforts has been breath-taking. People have called me, written me and even dropped in my office with the express purpose of complimenting me on my outspoken comments. There

seems to be one important element still lacking. People hesitate to stick their necks out and say what they think. This is understandable, considering the fact that some pretty important people might take offense at what they say. The old rule is "fools rush in where angels fear to tread," and it seems that I am the biggest fool in town.

He continued to talk about how "Republican powers that be" brag about "having controlled the postmaster job since the founding of the town (more than 50 years)" and he could understand why "appointment of a rabid Democrat like myself" would be opposed. However he did not know how they can "fight so hard against the best qualified applicant" no matter to which party he belongs. Pete had chosen his career so he was not campaigning for the position, but encouraged people to get more involved and to contact their Congressman. Even after his editorial, nothing changed with the status quo.

Boys Will be Boys

Pete's diligence, perseverance and reputation for being a "fighter for the underdog" spread quickly. Although I was not always aware who Pete represented in a court of law, in constructing and collecting stories from many hometown people, I have made new acquaintances from some who graduated before I did. I knew the names of many of them but did not know them personally.

A story I recently came across is one told by Dennie Crawford, who graduated in 1955. Dennie said he and some other high school boys were cited with tickets for loitering by a local police officer on a Saturday evening. Dennie's father contacted Pete.

Just because Pete was a young attorney and knew he may have

an uphill battle, he did not hesitate to contact "the big guns" if necessary. Of course that was before he gained a reputation of facing giants on his own. As a young child, I always knew who the Tulsa lawyer Thomas D. (Tommy) Frasier was, but was unaware of his status. I mainly remembered that Tommy Frasier was a paraplegic and a very capable attorney. Daddy contacted him. The municipal judge was taken aback as city court began and Tommy Frasier wheeled into the courtroom. The case was quickly dismissed for which Dennie and his dad were very grateful. Dennie was impressed with the strategy and skill of Daddy and Frasier. That stuck with Dennie all those years.

Another interesting story I heard a few years ago was told by Van Kunze. When he was a young teenager earning money baling hay with John Kinsey, he recalled they were baling on the MK & T right-of-way just west of Garnett Road one hot summer day. The baler kept breaking down and they had to keep stopping to unclog it. Mr. Kinsey was down inside the baler out of sight.

As inventive young boys will do, Van had taken a hat and attached goggles to it to be able to pull down when needed to keep the wind, dust and hay out of his eyes. He had learned to toss the hat outward with some action of his wrist and it would return to him similar to that of a boomerang. As he had done many times before, Van threw his hat up into the air expecting it to return to him in that circular motion he had seen so many times before. Much to his surprise, it kept going straight... straight into the windshield of a passing car which happened to be Pete Simmons' car. Pete slammed on his brakes and came to a sudden halt, jumping out of his car to reprimand this youngster as to the dangers of objects that could hinder a driver's view and thus resulting in an accident. About that time, Mr. Kinsey, a large, stocky man, heard the commotion and rose up out of the baler to see what was going on. Pete's eyes met Kinsey's. Since even on a good day, Pete only stood about five feet ten and a half inches tall, Van said he turned around and headed back to his car and went on his way. That story in itself was an unusual ending but Pete was wise enough to know he was far more adept in his verbal abilities than his physical ones. As a kid, Van mostly remembered the goggles, his creative invention broke when it hit the windshield.

The Truth and Nothing but the Truth

Pete always went to bat for the underdog, the underprivileged or children who did not have families or family support. John W. (J.W.) Scott is an example of that category. His story goes like this:

Both my parents died my junior year in high school. Mother died in November, 1953 and my father in April, 1954.

My granddad was named administrator of my affairs. A year later my granddad died and my grandmother was then named administrator.

About a year later it appeared that the task was a little more than she could handle. So Pete decided that we should go to court and have me declared legal age, even though I was only 18. When we went to court for the hearing, Pete called me up to testify. His goal was to show proof that I had not coerced my grandmother into seeking an adult status for me for the wrong reasons. By asking pertinent questions to me he was also trying to prove that I was not in the room when she signed the application or had prior knowledge of her motives. He asked me where I was when she signed the application.

I stated, "I was in your office." His face turned red and he sputtered.

But before he could say a word, I said, "But you and my grandmother had gone to another office so her signature could be witnessed." I think he would have killed me if we had not been in the courtroom!

He lectured me for hours that even though it was legal for me to buy beer at the time, that I had better not, or we would go out to the alley and discuss the matter! I still check to see if he is watching every time I buy beer, 59 years later! But that little piece of paper did great things for me. I could buy a new car and a pistol and best of all I got a marriage license, that has stood up for 56 years.

All I had to say was, "here read this" and I will admit it did get a little bit of beer, just to prove that I could!

First Employees

When Pete's office was first in his home, there was no need for a secretary. He took care of all the paperwork and details. Trying to consider who was actually Daddy's "first" but undoubtedly an "unpaid" secretary at 115 S. Main, I remember our mother working at the front desk occasionally. That may have been during the years that we lived in the back of his office. Having three children now to take care of, she probably only filled in when necessary. Although they had to cut costs during these times, there was still a certain amount of professionalism required to show that this law office and Broken Arrow's newest attorney is very capable of handling his client's business.

In the early 50's, I recall the very first "paid" secretary Daddy hired was Lottie Autry. She had attended Tulsa Business College after high school. Her son Bill said it may have been her first real job outside their home. Bill was about six or seven years old when his mother joined my dad's office. She no doubt gained some quick legal experience during the time she was there. When she left Pete's place, she worked for Cobb Motor Company on Main Street which was sold to Bradley Chevrolet. She followed Cobb over to his insurance company where she worked until he retired. Pete bought Ed Cobb's building and moved his law office there in 1957. At the time Mr. Cobb retired, Lottie went to Arkansas Valley Bank where she was the first teller at a drive up window.

Pete contacted Bill Autry about doing some concrete work for him. Bill had just left Bagby Harris, a ready mix concrete company in Jenks to start his own business. Bill and his finishing crew poured and finished the entire sidewalk on the south side of Pete's building between Main and the alley on El Paso.

Another lady I recall worked for Daddy in those early days was Viola Dill. I am not certain how long or how often she worked, but most people in town remember she later worked at Ross Drug Store. She had two daughters, Frances and Delores, and attended our church as did some of his other secretaries. Frances was one of our babysitters when we were young and she was in high school.

Business students and secretaries know that before computers were invented, we had to type on manual typewriters. There was no delete button so students attempted to do their best in having good typing skills with no errors. At the end of letters, one may recall, secretaries identified their work by typing their initials next to those of the one who dictated the letter to them.

Frances' husband, E.D. Loyd remembered a story that happened shortly after Viola began working for Pete. Pete may not have realized what her initials would look like until she typed her first letter for him, but he found something that was not really an error. She had typed in the bottom left corner their respective initials: PES/vd. He took the letter to her and said, "We're going to have to change something and come up with some different initials for you and not 'vd.'" I'm not for sure what they concluded. Maybe she had a middle initial that they used.

Along Came the High School Girls

Through the years he trained many secretaries, most of whom were still in high school. Shirley Sherrell Kates was one of the first high school girls who worked for Pete after school. She recalls: "You know I was probably the first young girl to work in his office, just answering the phone and typing up legal stuff. And sometimes babysitting you kids. You were so tiny and cute. Happy all the time."

Susanne (Sudie) Sherrell Cypert and Peggy Sherrell Van-Dyke were Shirley's younger sisters who also received their secretarial training in Pete's office at 115 S. Main.

Sudie remembers Pete being her Sunday School teacher in the ninth grade. Her mother was widowed and Sudie was very grateful that Pete gave her the opportunity to earn money and also helped pay for her college courses. She kept a letter that Daddy had written to Northeastern State College on her behalf and gave it to me recently. There was a special place in Pete's heart for widows and orphans. Mrs. Sherrell eventually married John Tucker, Connie and Tommy Tucker's father who also attended church with us.

"Several of his Sunday School students were his high school secretaries, from the Methodist Church," Connie Tucker Collins reminded me. Karen Jennings Treat mentioned that Mildred (Millie) Cobb was included in the group of high school girls from

PAUL E. SIMMONS
Attorney at Law
112 South Main
BROKEN ARROW, OKLA.

September 15, 1958

Northeastern State College
Placement Service
Tahlequah, Oklahoma

Dear Sirs:

I have been personally acquainted with Susanne Grace Sherrell for approximately ten years. I was her Sunday School teacher when she was in Jr. High School. I am familiar with her reputation in the community of Broken Arrow, Oklahoma, and know her reputation to be superior. She is an active member of the First Methodist Church of Broken Arrow, and her character is above reproach.

Susanne was employed by me, as a part-time secretary, after school and on week-ends, while she was in high school. I have absolutely nothing but praise for her as an employee. I found her to be efficient, diligent, honest, loyal and of good personality. I feel that she is trustworthy and capable of acquitting herself well in any position for which she has been trained.

Susanne left my employ to continue her education. I would have no hesitation in hiring her again or in giving her any further recommendation which may be required or desired.

Yours very truly,

Paul E. Simmons

PES:mrs

Sudie saved Pete's recommendation letter for college,
and still had it after 60 years.

the church and probably worked after the Sherrell girls left.

Other sisters who worked for Pete were Shirley Lemon Ingold and Carolyn Lemon Keele, the daughters of Paul and Inez Lemon, a family name that is readily recognized in Broken Arrow. As some girls graduated, others would take their places, eager to use their acquired skills they had learned in their business office classes in high school.

Following In Pete's Footsteps

As young girls look up to and admire older girls in high school, I was no different. One of my favorite high school girls was Marcella Burgess Giles who was actually only a few years older than I. At a school reunion a few years ago, I had an opportunity to visit with Marcella the evening prior to a Pioneer Dinner. As an introductory question to Marcella, I inquired if she "had been scared of Pete as much as I was when I worked in his office."

With a laugh, she replied, "Of course not, I got my bluff in on him quickly. He was really good to work for and taught me a lot. As a matter of fact, his inspiration and motivation led me to become a lawyer myself." I might add that Marcella is currently a lawyer for the Bureau of Indian Affairs in Washington, D.C. The most important thing that I took away from my conversation with her was to think how extremely proud Pete would have been of Marcella if he had been alive to hear that.

Secretaries Who Had Dual Roles

As previously mentioned, it is obvious the young ladies who Daddy trained as secretaries had babysitting skills so we knew them on a personal level as well. One of my personal favorites was Mary Ruth Roberts Megee, who rode the bus to high school with the kids from the Lynn Lane area although she only lived as far north as 61st Street. She recalls she came to work at the law office because our fathers knew each other. She had such a sweet personality and was so kind. After she and Russell Megee married, I remember them living on Toledo in Arrow Heights. Although we three Simmons children were actually babysat often by Mary Ruth, I only recall one particular evening. She told me one afternoon we arrived at the Megee home, she cooked a meal and none of us would eat it. I found that difficult to believe because I was not a picky eater. I wondered if we had already eaten our evening meal, but she said we had not. So she asked us what we wanted and she finally found something for us that we accepted. This event may have occurred before Pete gave us the speech about "being grateful for what we have." It is unusual how people remember different things about the same situation. What made that evening a special memory for me was the introduction to making Snickerdoodle cookies.

Mary Ruth also recalled a very peculiar thing Pete did every spring around Easter time. He was in the habit of giving up smoking for the Lenten season. He chose that vice to lay aside every year. I remember that also. She said it did not appear that it was very difficult a task from which to abstain, which I had also observed. But his answer to her when she inquired was "If I quit smoking, I wouldn't have anything to give up for Lent."

Among the other favorite young ladies who graced Pete's office were Lanell Nichols Copeland and Jean Davis Poplin, who have unfortunately passed on at this writing. I had several conversations with Jean at numerous Pioneer Dinners about getting "Pete's girls" together in a group picture at one of the Pioneer Dinners. Sadly, that did not happen. I am still hopeful that we can have a group picture of Daddy's secretaries someday.

A Growing Family

The summer after my fourth grade school year in 1957, we moved to 703 E. Ft. Worth, a home in Haskell Addition. That fall Barbara and I attended Southside Elementary School after I had already attended North Main for four years prior. Chris continued school at North Main for his seventh grade. We caught the bus right outside our front door at the corner of Ft.

Worth and 6th Street. Looking back now, it may have seemed like a long bus ride, but it only took us from close to the corner of 81st and Lynn Lane to 81st and Elm Place, a full mile away. As I am sure some readers can relate to, when remembering events from the perspective of a child, we did not realize that many of the schools and places we lived through the years were actually outside the original town site of Broken Arrow.

Our family had grown and Daddy had need for a separate room in the house to use as an office when clients came for consultation after regular work hours. Broken Arrow continued to grow and make room for families moving here because of the expansion of Braden Winch and American Airlines. One of the first neighbors I was welcomed by was Rose Ann Hurst, whose dad had transferred here because of American Airlines. Her brothers Billy and Tony were younger. Neighborhoods were safe then and we rarely locked our doors. We played "kick the can" under the streetlight during the summer time. Friends my age and Barbara's were Patty Jones, Greg Dodd, Susan Taylor, Carolyn Jackson, Carolyn Vaughan, Susan Dobbins and the Deed Dobbins family. Other neighbors Chris' age or older were Tommy Reed, Ray Jackson and Larry Pennington. We could generally remember what street as well as in which house each of our friends lived. Even some of our teachers who would shudder to think their students knew where they lived but knew their property was safe were Mrs. Eudora Reed and Coach Ron McHenry.

The field just south of us was overgrown and barren. We used it as a baseball field with our Haskell Addition friends as well as some of our neighboring friends who lived close like Arlie and Dennis McIntire. Larry Pennington who became a local realtor in Broken Arrow recalls:

I grew up in the same neighborhood with the Simmons

children. Pete's son, Chris and I graduated from Broken Arrow High School together. Behind their home was a vacant field, so all the neighborhood boys got together and built a baseball field. We spent several summers playing ball on our baseball field. In the course of playing baseball we would get thirsty and hungry. Since the Simmons home was next door, we would ask for something to drink. Mrs. Simmons would always find something for us. It was during those summer days that I got to know Pete and his wife.

Later that field became Blue Star Addition which my dad affectionately called the B.S. Addition because the developer built smaller homes than Haskell Addition's. They were closer together and lowered our property value. Pete never shirked back from stating his personal opinions. His statements did not leave much to guesswork.

Many of our friends and neighbors may have contacted our dad for legal services, but I was not aware of it. Even friends from high school told me years later that Pete was their attorney, but our dad had a code of ethics, loyalty and privacy.

Carnival Time

Days on Main Street of Broken Arrow in the 1950's were active. At one time there were so many cotton gins in our growing town they had a yearly activity in town called Cotton Jubilee. It was a time to celebrate the successfulness of their crops. Farmers would bring the harvest of their cotton crops to town on that day to sell. A carnival came to town and there were rides set up. A few years later it became Rooster Day as the farmers would come to town on one particular day that was set aside for them to sell or exchange their roosters for others. The carnival rides continued. One of my biggest joys and memories is that some of the carnival rides were set up right squarely in front of Daddy's office as they spread up to Broadway and down past Commercial on Rooster Day every year, with the bandstand in the middle of Commercial and Main Street. Most business offices may have been closed for the event, but Pete's office was open that morning of Rooster Day at least until noon. He always took advantage of being available to conduct his business as usual, but we kids were more concerned about having fun riding the rides. I'm sure like most children growing up in the 1940s, we took our father's hard work and support too much for granted. He did not take his job lightly. He was driven to succeed and serve.

From Cotton Jubilee to Rooster Day,
Broken Arrow has always enjoyed celebrating the success of
local businesses. -- Tracey Hunsecker, Jr. and Andy Chisolm, owner of
Lindy's cafe, pose with a rooster while getting ready
for this year's Rooster Day. ca. 1952.
• Courtesy of Broken Arrow Historical Museum, Broken Arow Oklahoma
• Used by permission The Tulsa Word, Tulsa, Oklahoma

Pete was the chairman of the committee that named
Haskell Elementary School in Broken Arrow, Oklahoma.
• Courtesy of Patty Stegall Maupin

Chapter 13
NAMING A NEW BROKEN ARROW SCHOOL - CONTROVERSY

A story of my parents being involved in an interesting tale related to the "naming of a new school" in the late 1950s was shared with me by Dr. Clarence G. Oliver, Jr. In our joint preparation of this Chapter, Dr. Oliver broadened my knowledge of Broken Arrow Public Schools and the community. Reading this story, I believe you will see the same pattern in almost every circumstance in which Pete is involved and also enjoy a bit humor about small town politics.

An initial surge of the approximately 1,300 people arrived to establish the new Broken Arrow, Indian Territory, community in 1902-1903. After statehood in 1907, there was only modest growth for much of the town's first half-Century. The population reached a high point of 2,086 by the time the 1920

Broken Arrow Public School was on Main Street, (1903) Indian Territory until destroyed by fire damage in 1919.
• Courtesy of Broken Arrow Historical Museum

census was recorded, but dropped back to 1,900 people during the years of the "Great Depression" and had almost returned to its 1920 population level by 1940 and the start of World War II.

Broken Arrow Historical Society records indicate that more than

400 Broken Arrowans were serving in the military during the war years. With the end of World War II in 1945, veterans from the area returned to Broken Arrow to rejoin their established families. By 1950, the community's population reached 3,000, with the increase being young school age children.

One school building had served as the "Broken Arrow School" from 1903 until 1919, housing students of all grades. When the State Legislature failed to continue funding for the short-lived Haskell Agricultural College that was established in 1909 and closed 10 years later, the community inherited the college campus and building. The most prominent building was an impressive three-story brick structure which had been the college's main classroom facility. That campus became the second school site for Broken Arrow. The Junior High School and High School students attended that campus. The original school building (1903) was replaced in 1924 because of lighting strike, fire damage and building deterioration. The newly constructed Main Street School (1924) became the Grade School. Those two school facilities were very adequate for the student population until the mid-1950s after the end of the Korean War when new families began to move to Broken Arrow. The next five years would bring a population surge that would challenge and change Broken Arrow.

A new housing addition was proposed "way out south of town," as some people described the project. The houses would be more than a mile from downtown Broken Arrow. The new addition, named "Arrow Heights," was the first development to be built outside the original Broken Arrow town site boundary of 1902.

G. L. (Glyn Loyd) Hollabaugh, who had a successful career at East Central and Union, became the Broken Arrow Superintendent of Schools in 1944. Superintendent Hollabaugh persuaded the Board of Education that one new school building would be needed immediately and one or two additional schools would be needed in the next five or six years. A small acreage of land was

"Haskell Agricultural College (1909-1919) became Broken Arrow's Junior and Senior High School building when the town outgrew the building on Main Street. Pete recalled the third floor was the study hall classroom.
• Courtesy of Broken Arrow Historical Museum, Broken Arrow, Oklahoma

purchased across the street from the southwest corner of town, West Houston Street and South Elm Place, and the school district voters were asked to approve a bond issue to build a new school, to be named "Southside Elementary School." That school was built in 1954 and consisted of eight classrooms, a small cafeteria and offices. Most of the students would be "bused" to Southside from the new "Arrow Heights" housing development that was being constructed a mile south of the school site.

Two years later, as Superintendent Hollabaugh had expected, another elementary school was needed to serve students in the north part of Broken Arrow where new houses were being constructed in several smaller additions. Those also were "just outside" the community's original town site boundary.

School district voters approved another bond issue in 1956 to build a school slightly larger than the Southside School. The new school was located on East Midway Street, a block south of the newly-designated State Highway 51 that now extended east along Tulsa County's 71st Street. This school contained 12 classrooms, a small cafeteria and offices. Superintendent Hollabaugh and the School Board decided to name this new school "Northeast Elementary School."

Broken Arrow's population continued to increase as more new families sought houses in what was becoming a very popular "suburban" community for the Tulsa metropolitan area. The city's population was about to reach the 5,000 mark. More new housing additions were planned in the south and east areas of the city. Plans were being made for the third elementary school. The Board of Education purchased 10 acres of land "out in the country" on the northwest corner of the intersection of South Lynn Lane Road and 81st Street. Even though the bond issue hadn't been finalized and plans were still being made, school leaders were already discussing the new school by the name, "Southeast Elementary School."

Clarence G. Oliver, Jr., moved his young family to Broken Arrow in 1955 to accept a position as an English and Journalism teacher at Broken Arrow High School. He returned to his earlier career field of Journalism and was managing editor of the Broken Arrow Ledger at the time the Northeast Elementary School was opened. He had grown up in a community where schools were named after famous people in the nation or community; and, he felt that giving "directional names" to schools was not a good policy.

Oliver attended Irving Grade School in Ada, Oklahoma, an historic school that was named after the famous American author Washington Irving and was a school that had been attended not only by Oliver's mother, but also by Robert S. Kerr, who later became an Oklahoma Governor and long-time United States Senator, and by Oral Roberts, who later became one of the world's best known radio and television evangelists and who established Oral Roberts University.

During the time the Northeast Elementary School was being constructed, and was "named," Editor Oliver had written a few newspaper editorials in which he expressed an opinion about the use of "directional names" for schools and suggesting that "people names" would be more appropriate. When the discussion started about the proposed "Southeast Elementary School," Oliver returned to that "school naming" topic and wrote additional editorials in which he suggested that the Board of Education choose some national hero or other person of historical significance as the name for the planned new elementary school.

Superintendent Hollabaugh, who had employed Oliver in 1955 as a teacher and also to assist with school public relations and news activities, decided to "do something" to counter the editorial criticism.

Earlier, Editor Oliver had assisted Superintendent Hollabaugh, who had been appointed by Governor Raymond Gary to serve on the Oklahoma State Board of Education, in writing and publishing what was Oklahoma's first set of recommended "School District Policies." That innovative project was partially funded by a small grant that Superintendent Hollabaugh had been able to obtain. The Superintendent and Editor were good friends, active members of First Baptist Church, Broken Arrow, and in the Broken Arrow Chamber of Commerce. The two friends obviously disagreed on how school buildings should be named. And, the Board of Education did not have any policy concerning such matters.

Superintendent Hollabaugh told Editor Oliver, "Okay, you win," adding that the Board of Education was "appointing a committee" to develop a recommended policy concerning naming future schools, and "you are on the committee." The Board of Education appointed Attorney Paul (Pete) Simmons to serve as Chairman, included Dorothy Cline, Broken Arrow Parent-Teacher Association President, and Oliver as members.

"Members of Broken Arrow School Board and faculty planning the 1955-56 school year, Left to Right: *Glyn L. Hollabaugh, Superintendent, Archie Gwartney, Principal of North Side Grade School, J.M. Friggel, Lee N. Walker, Elmer Loyd, A.B. Cheatham, Mike Simmons."*
• Used by Permission Broken Arrow Ledger and Broken Arrow Historical Museum

Superintendent Hollabaugh and members of the Board of Education recognized Simmons as a "history buff" with great knowledge of Oklahoma's history. He had the legal expertise which would be valuable in recommending official school district policy. The other committee members agreed that Simmons was the most appropriate choice. Since the committee would be meeting in the homes of committee members, the three spouses—Frances Simmons, Vinita Oliver and Clyde Cline—were considered unofficial committee members who would be sitting in on the committee meetings as the group drank coffee, ate cookies, and talked about a variety of ideas related to "naming schools."

At one of the meetings, Frances Simmons suggested the use of Oklahoma's Governors starting with Charles N. Haskell, the state's first Governor. Haskell's name already had a Broken Arrow connection. The former Haskell Agricultural School in Broken Arrow was named in his honor. Nearby was the community's Haskell Pond, a small lake that had been a favorite picnic area, fishing spot, ice-skating location during winter months, and had been located on the Haskell College farmland since 1909. Also, the new proposed "Southeast Elementary School" site was at the edge of what had at one time been part of the Haskell College farmland.

Haskell had been active in the effort to bring Indian Territory into the Union as the planned new State of Sequoyah and had served as a delegate and elected Vice President to the Sequoyah Constitutional Convention in 1905. When the two Territories (Indian and Oklahoma) were forced to become "one state," Haskell was chosen to serve on the Constitutional Convention for the new State of Oklahoma. He was an extremely popular leader and was elected as Governor in 1907 by a very high vote margin.

Thus, the committee voted the new Broken Arrow school be named "Charles N. Haskell Elementary School" and that a policy be developed to name all future schools after Oklahoma's Governors, choosing names in sequence of service. Thus, future schools would be named after Lee Cruce, R. L. Williams, James B. A. Robertson, Jack Walton, and continuing in sequence. The committee believed it was appropriate to remove former Governors who had been impeached. The school board members would make that decision.

Committee Chairman Paul E. (Pete) Simmons prepared the written policy recommendation for the Board of Education. He and the committee members appeared at the next regular meeting of the Board of Education and presented the committee report, suggesting that the new school be named the "Charles N. Haskell Elementary School" and recommending that future schools be named after Oklahoma's Governors, with names chosen on basis of sequence of service. The Board's response was not what the committee members expected.

Immediately, "Politics" raised its head.

"We are not going to name Broken Arrow's new schools after a bunch of Democrat Governors," one board member sternly stated.

The committee members had not considered the political party affiliation of the Governors. It was true. All were Democrats. And, all the members of the Board of Education were Republicans. The first Republican Governor was not elected until Governor Henry Bellmon, who took office in 1963. Pete Simmons probably knew about the political registration of the Governors, but that had not been a point of discussion during committee meetings.

After much discussion by Superintendent Hollabaugh and school board members, a decision was made to accept the name, "Charles N. Haskell Elementary School," instead of "Southeast Elementary School" which had been previously considered. School board members advised the committee that the Haskell name was acceptable because of the historical connections of the former Haskell College, the Haskell Pond, and the location of the new school site on the former Haskell College farmland. But, the idea of using names of Oklahoma's Governors for future schools was rejected.

"Your committee is now dissolved," Superintendent Hollabaugh told Simmons and the other members.

The name of the new school was embraced by Superintendent Hollabaugh. He resigned as superintendent in 1959 and asked to be assigned as the first principal at the newly constructed Charles N. Haskell Elementary School. Hollabaugh later served briefly as an accreditation officer with the Oklahoma State Department of Education, and retired in 1965.

Hollabaugh died in September 1993, at the age of 92.

"Honoring Dr. Glyn L. (G.L.) Hollabaugh for his service to Broken Arrow Public Schools with 'This is Your Life' presentation on March 6, 1959)
• Courtesy of Broken Arrow Historical Museum

*'Pete' Simmons, young ambitious lawyer ready
to meet the needs of his hometown clients.*

Chapter 14
MOVIN' ON UP
TO THE SOUTH END OF MAIN

The fall of 1957, Pete finalized the purchase of Ed Cobb's building and moved into a new office at 323 S. Main Street of Broken Arrow. The building is located on the northeast corner of Main and El Paso caddy corner from our current Broken Arrow Historical Museum and extended all the way to alley with opportunity to rent out the other offices facing El Paso. Mother decorated the office with a modern settee and chairs of beige with a triangular table that she had chosen from a selection of office furniture at the Sears store at 21st and Yale in Tulsa. How well I remember Mother working part time at Sears for those few months up to Christmastime in order to pay for that furniture. It may have been in layaway for awhile prior to opening the new office. Louise Wilson worked with Mother that fall and they knew they were accomplishing their goals, whether it was Christmas gifts, furniture or other merchandise.

After the office was established awhile, Daddy contacted Pauline Unruh with whom he had visited on our trip to Alaska in 1959. She came to work for him. She had quite a bit of experience working for a law firm in Anchorage, so Mrs. Unruh added a lot to the knowledge and expertise of the one-lawyer firm.

In 1960, Arvle N. Lewis, a local insurance agent told Yvonne Satterfield Morgan, (originally from the Porter area) that Pete Simmons was looking for a new secretary because Mrs. Unruh was moving back to Alaska. She received a phone call from Pete. Yvonne and her sister were working downtown Tulsa for Sanders

The Life and Career of Paul E. "Pete" Simmons

and McAnally's law firm. She remembers Pete telling her if she could work for a 'son-of-a-gun' like Sanders, he knew she could work for him without difficulty. After considering leaving a position she enjoyed with her sister, but also thinking it would be nice not having to drive all the way to Tulsa, she agreed to quit that firm and come to work for Pete. Once she told David Sanders the situation, he offered her a raise and changed her hours to match those of her husband's James. James worked for the downtown Tulsa Post Office so they could ride to work together. She decided to stay on with the Tulsa firm for the difference in pay and hours.

When her daughter Jamie was a year old in July of 1963, Yvonne finally came to work in Broken Arrow at Pete's office on South Main. She could hardly believe the difference between the two atmospheres. She said compared to the Tulsa firm, Pete's Broken Arrow office was casual and relaxed. She remembered it as totally laid back. However, on her first day she realized Pete accomplished a lot of work in a short amount of time as she assisted in the legal documents of four divorces. She learned quickly to take dictation the way Daddy dictated letters over Mary Ruth Megee's shoulder about ten years earlier.

Yvonne took a leave of absence when her second child, Scott was born in February, 1965, but returned in January, 1967 working half days when Scott was two years old. Yvonne was there through most of the other law associates who came and went through the years.

Simmons Overwhelms Fallis

One of Daddy's most important but grueling cases was a young Broken Arrow man charged with rape. The case was important to Daddy because the young man's life and future was at stake. He had a policy with his clients. He told them, "Don't ever lie to me so I'll know how to represent you." He wanted his clients to be able to trust him but also wanted to be able to trust what his clients told him as well. I do not know the ages of the young man or the alleged victim. His client assured him he was not guilty. The client told Daddy she was promiscuous and blatantly lied about him. The young man also had a couple of friends who knew and had dated the young lady. The friends said the same thing.

The day of the trial Daddy's client was joined with several other high school boys who testified on his client's behalf. The team of prosecuting attorneys headed up by District Attorney S.M. "Buddy" Fallis could not prove the young man's guilt so he was declared innocent.

Within a few days, Daddy's client came to give Pete a special gift. It was a little statue with an engraved sign: "Simmons Over-whelms Fallis." That gift, a sign of accomplishment against the odds, was as important to Daddy as collecting a fee.

Mentoring Young Lawyers

As it had been Pete's vow in 1950 as a young lawyer, he was determined to give back to the community and mentor young lawyers who were seeking a start in their profession. One of the first attorneys to work in Pete's office was George Park, who came in 1963. After he had some experience under his belt,

Robert 'Bob' with baby Ashley

he partnered with David Nelson at the corner of Commercial and Ash. He later moved to an office on Kenosha.

The next young lawyer for Yvonne and Pete to "break in" and my favorite was Robert "Bob" Stubblefield. Bob, Dorothy Simmons' son-in-law, was a graduate of Tulsa Central High School. He had just graduated from college in 1964 and was getting ready to enter law school at the University of Tulsa. Dorothy introduced Bob to Daddy and with jubilance Pete replied, "Come see me when you get out of law school. I may have a place for you."

I believe that Pete was always fond of Bob Stubblefield too because he recognized a hard worker when he saw one. Once he knew Bob was working nights and attending school during the day, it must have reminded him of his own early days in law school. Seeing a diligent young man with integrity and a good work ethic, Pete knew Bob would be a successful attorney and worthy of mentoring.

Others discovered the potential in Bob's abilities. Robert L. "Bob" Kinkaid was the current Tulsa County Commissioner at the time. Kinkaid, a Republican, was an independent oil man who enjoyed politics. He searched out young law students with good grades and gave them job opportunities. He hired Bob Stubblefield to work with the maintenance crew at the Tulsa County Court House. Bob was appreciative even though the hours were long— 4:30 p.m. to 12:00 a.m. He would get off work and have to be in class at TU at 8:00 a.m. sharp.

Stubblefield graduated and joined Pete's law office in the fall of 1968. Bob said he was thrown into the ring for his "on the job training" when he was still wet behind the ears. As his first case alone, Pete sent him down to Coweta to appear before the Justice of the Peace in November of that year. "Now, Bob," Pete began. "The J.P. will probably find your client guilty, so when he makes the judgment, you just tell him you want to appeal to the court in Wagoner."

It was a cold fall morning when Bob arrived in Coweta to appear before the J.P. There was an open stove in the courtroom to warm the room. Just as Pete had predicted, the J.P. found his client guilty. So just as instructed, Bob replied, "I hereby give notice to appeal." The J.P. was taken aback and said, "Appeal?" Bob stood his ground and left. The next day the J.P. called Pete so he in turn stepped around the corner to Bob's office and announced that Bob's case was dismissed. Pete reminded Bob to not be afraid and don't back down. Bob had a lot more training of that kind. He said he gained a lot of good common sense training from Pete.

Bob told me he was impressed by Pete's mentorship. "Pete never pretended to be an expert or a lawyer who specialized in just one area of law." He admired Pete's knack for how much he accomplished each day. He said that Pete would start off the day examining an abstract. Then he would do the paperwork for an adoption, followed by working on documents for an oil lease. That afternoon he would go to Tulsa and move from a jury trial to a divorce case later in the day. Although people have perceived Pete as a small town lawyer, they recognized he knew his law and could perform in the courtroom as easily as any other competent uptown attorney. He felt the reason clients were at ease discussing their problems and situations with Pete is he was not rushed and took the time to listen to them and truly cared about them.

Bob shared because the laws are so complicated now, it would virtually be impossible to not specialize in certain areas of law. He said most laws for drawing up a will are the same, but so much has been changed in family law, it would be difficult for one lawyer to keep up with all the updates in order to meet the needs of clients in several different areas.

Other new attorneys who began their careers at his office or developed them with Daddy's mentoring were Jack Ross, Bob Funston, Joe Fallin and G. Lee Jackson. Of these four young attorneys I remember Bob Funston and Jack Ross best.

Robert (Bob) Funston came after Robert (Bob) Stubblefield. By this time, Stubblefield was well aware of Pete's antics, so now it was time to properly break Funston in. The initiation to this law firm was to see if one could handle the humor and jokes from the senior lawyer when least expecting it. Daddy always had nicknames for lots of people. Yvonne reminded me recently Daddy had pet names for the two Roberts. Robert and Bob may have been used interchangeably with them. But just as Peter and Paul became Pete and Emmett Earl for his brother Earl, Pete was eager to create new nicknames for his young guns. Since one was Robert Louis Funston and the other was Robert Joe Stubblefield, they became Bobby Lou and Bobby Joe. I do not know how they felt about their nicknames, but they probably tolerated it very well.

Bob Funston was an ambitious young man and eventually became our State Senator. After his term of office expired he remained in the Oklahoma City area. Robert Stubblefield remembers Funston as being a very intelligent and capable attorney.

Not Exactly Abraham Lincoln

Once when Bob Funston was practicing law in Daddy's office he brought to Pete's attention a plaque Daddy had above his office door, which quoted Abraham Lincoln: *"A lawyer's time and advice are his stock in trade."*

Bob challenged Pete on whether or not he really believed that. Daddy always valued his clients enough to allow them the time they needed. People did not have to make an appointment ahead of time. They could call or come into the office. If he was not in a court session, Daddy was working at the office. He gave clients his full attention. He never charged for a consultation.

Bob explained his interpretation of the plaque was a lawyer's time and advice was as if he were on the clock working at a regular 8 to 5 job. He would get paid for his time and services. Daddy told Bob he absolutely refused to charge clients an hourly fee. After the conversation, Daddy took the sign down. As much as Pete admired Abraham Lincoln, he stood firm in his principles. It was more important to him to assist his clients than to receive a fee for services.

Another time, the two attorneys feuded about issues in a the presidential election and finally drew a "proverbial" line down the middle of their law office with duct tape until after the election.

Continuing to Fight for Justice

(Bobby) Nick Hood, Jr. and his wife Janice (Mallow) Hood told me how Daddy helped Janice's parents, Mr. and Mrs. Mallow, in a legal matter. When the Mallows returned from California, they lost all of their personal belongings in a trailer by fire. Nick and Janice remembered Pete fighting to recover the full amount of the cost of their goods, right down to the very last dollar.

Perry Mason and Della Street

The more Daddy liked a person, the more likely one was to be given a nickname. One of our favorite shows to watch during the old black and white days of television was Perry Mason. Daddy liked to take the challenge of solving the mystery before this famous fictitious character did on the screen, or so it would appear.

Mason had a very competent legal secretary who was at his beck and call. She was Della Street. Daddy began calling Yvonne Della. She was very patient and kind and probably laughed and enjoyed Pete's humor. Yvonne's favorite story about this nickname is one her neighbor told her. Her neighbor apparently babysat for a man who was one of Daddy's clients. He once referred to Yvonne's neighbor by her nickname. Not having heard the story before, her neighbor corrected him and told him Mr. Simmons' secretary is Yvonne Morgan. He was totally convinced her name was Della because he had heard with his own ears Pete call her Della! I believe he finally understood the whole story but not until the neighbor explained it. We laughed about that story then and even more now.

Nearby Businesses

Pete Simmons' law office on South Main was unsophisticated and unorthodox. When Daddy stopped long enough for lunch, he wanted everyone to enjoy lunch too. Yvonne recently asked me if I remembered the little grocery store Stanfill's had.

Stanfills had a grocery store and dress shop on Main Street. They built a small lunch stand in the alley near Ash and Broadway. During the summer, Pete would send one of us up to the lunch stand to get food for all of us. It was an old-fashioned lunch counter. One could order lunch meat, cheese and other condiments there. Daddy's choice was bologna, cheddar cheese which Daddy affectionately called "rat cheese." He always got black olives for Mother. Yvonne said that was the summer she learned to like black olives.

Daddy's building which once belonged to Mr. Ed Cobb had a variety of offices located in it as well as an upstairs apartment. Yvonne remembered Berniece Crain and her mom, Bitha

Bodewig living there for awhile. Berniece told me recently Daddy helped them when they had no place to go. Leona Brown had a beauty shop on El Paso. She had moved from working in Kathryn Wheeler's shop above Jones' Drug to this location. Several ladies came for their weekly hairdos, Virginia Johnson from Arkansas Valley Bank, Wilma Shanks and Virginia Brown both came from Nelson Ford.

Of course the Tag Agency was at the end of the building right next to the alley. This whole row of businesses gave our high school girls and young mothers an opportunity to work while their children were in school.

Moving On

After the young lawyers who worked with Pete were established with their new practices and clients, they were ready to move on. Jack Ross bought Pete's firm between 1969 and 1970 but Daddy still owned the building. Ivan Brown had contacted Jack to be Arkansas Valley Bank's attorney. Funston was involved in politics and Stubblefield joined a Tulsa firm, eventually becoming a criminal lawyer. There were other lawyers who came and left during those times. It was time for a chapter to end and another one to begin at Main and El Paso in Broken Arrow.

THEY BROUGHT HOME SECOND PLACE HONORS - Members of the Broken Arrow delegation to the Oklahoma Community achievement banquet in Oklahoma City. Posing with Gov. Dewey Bartlett; Scott Graham, Pete Simmons, and C.A. McWilliams accepting the award.

Chapter 15
COMMUNITY INVOLVEMENT

When Pete returned from the Marine Corps, he took community service seriously. He was active in Chamber of Commerce, VFW, American Legion and later Broken Arrow's Optimist Club. He was often a guest speaker for various occasions. He was invited to speak for ARGO, an organization in Tulsa perhaps before law school with which I was not familiar.

Master Sergeant Pete Simmons

He has been, for 16 months, on Beauganville and Guadalcanal… and it's thru the courtesy of 'Sally' Bringham that we will have him with us at our next meeting.
We suggest you be present and hear about some of the things our boys are doing down in the Southwest Pacific. Sally tells us that it will be most interesting.

I would imagine even as a child, if Pete could draw an audience, he could and often did perform. He was gifted in his quick wit, able to learn things either quickly or by perseverance and seemed to have an inner knowing or presence of mind.
He once told me he first broke his nose when he fell off his tricycle head-first. The second time was when he was climbing a tree and fell out of it. He said his Grandma Neighbors commented as he shook off the dizziness and climbed that tree again, "that Paul has such a presence of mind".
He taught himself several little tricks he considered unique,

like riding a bicycle backwards. Again, if I had any reason to doubt his far-fetched stories, either I had an opportunity to see him act it out or I found a picture in a box years later.

Once a Clown, Always a Clown

Throughout our elementary years, we spent our time on the carnival rides and the midway playing games during Rooster Day. Daddy could not even ride the ferris wheel because his equilibrium made him nauseous. But once we started riding horses, we had a hobby Pete enjoyed and could participate in. Because we did not live on a farm or even the country, the first place we kept our horses was at Crockett's farm where Oak Crest Addition is now located on South Main. Other families like the Friends, Browns, Harrigers, Halls, Bright, Clays and Galls rented stalls and kept their horses there too. It was very convenient to ride our horses through the pasture to Lynn Lane to the Broken Arrow Rodeo grounds.

Rodeos were held throughout the year but our big event was Rooster Day Rodeo. Pete did not rope or ride bulls, but he always made himself useful in the arena. Several of the men would assist the riders and be observant for their safety. There were hired clowns who would not only provide entertainment but allow the rider to safely exit the arena while they distracted the bull. Apparently that activity attracted Pete because before long, he was out in the arena with the regular clown helping the riders escape possible injury. Except instead of being in painted make-up and in full regalia, he would sometimes come directly from the office or court in his suit clothes to participate. It is not that he did not have the time, just that he probably would not take the time to change clothes. Most often Pete was in his dungarees, ready for action. Kathy Friend Brumley, one of our many Broken Arrow

Round Up Club Queens reminded me of Pete being dressed in his suit clothes instead of blue jeans. This rodeo activity and hobby of his pointed out again that he liked helping people but if he could add a little humor to their lives, it was very fulfilling to him.

Wesley Sunday School Class

Over the course of thirty-five years, Daddy taught Sunday School to various age groups. The most memorable was The Wesley Sunday School Class at First Methodist Church. It was a very close-knit group through the years. Some of the members were Hoil and Mahala Thompson, Wayne and Virginia Brown, O.T. (Andy) and Doris Anderson, Lewis and Evelyn Spradling, Dr. James and Donna Newcomb and many others.

Hoil and Mahala Thompson had been friends from the moment they moved to Broken Arrow. They not only were members of his Sunday School class, but Daddy performed their daughter, Karen's wedding ceremony at their home in Wagoner County in 1979.

One lesson that Doris Anderson told me she believed was one of Daddy's best lessons to teach was during the Easter season. It was the enumeration of all the atrocities made against Jesus during his trial. It was before books and commentaries were published and the many movies that were made about Jesus' trial and crucifixion. She said as a lawyer, he brought out the legal aspect of the trial she felt as no one else could do. I remember Daddy studying and reviewing his Sunday School lesson.

Daddy enjoyed explaining the Greek word for Holy Spirit whose name actually means "advocate" or "one who goes along side" to his Wesley Sunday School Class. He shared with them it has a deeper meaning still. He also brought in the legal aspect and helped people visualize a scenario that one cannot even approach the "bench" or enter into the presence of a king if one does not know, or have a relationship with the one in supreme authority. He taught the function of the Holy Spirit was like having proper representation and grace or favor. He brought the subject full circle by sharing that a lawyer in a court of law is an advocate.

Methodist Men

Platform: *Clyde Cline, Paul E. Simmons, unknown, unknown,*
Front Row: *unknown, Harold Murray, Sr., John Hartman, Jim Rieb, Harold Murray, Jr., Bill Lester, unknown, unknown*
Second Row: *unknown, unknown, Philip Harman, George Wild, Wilbur Parrish, R.D. Patterson, unknown, Barney Cheek*
Third Row: *Harry Linell, Jr., unknown, Hugh Coshow, unknown, Robert "Bob" Steinberg, Sr. Richard "Dick" Steinberg, Robert "Bob" Steinberg, Jr.*

Along with teaching Sunday School he was active in the Methodist Men's group at church. I found in his file a picture that was probably taken during the early to mid-1960's in the old sanctuary built in 1924. It was most likely a Methodist Men's meeting because there were no women in the picture except our church organist, Jean Hartman.

Methodist Youth Fellowship (MYF)

Both Daddy and Mother at one time were sponsors of our Methodist Youth Fellowship (MYF) group on Sunday evenings. These were times before our churches had youth pastors. Teenagers are not always the easiest age group to teach, much less hold their attention for an hour. But my friends still remember how much they enjoyed coming to our youth group. Some of our friends who were in our class or came as guests were Lana Cross, Myrna Wair, Stan and Alan Keller, David Hartman, Donnie Anderson, Rita Fulps, Billie Sue Reynolds and Paula Dearstone. Of course, during our break and fellowship after the class, Daddy always entertained the kids with some of his tricks. Billie Sue reminded me one trick she liked. He would hold one leg straight out in front of him and quickly jump over it. It doesn't sound difficult but one must be agile, quick and with good balance to accomplish that.

It was about this time my friends started calling my parents Pete and Gladys from the popular television show at the time starring Harry Morgan. Daddy liked for everyone to just call him Pete. So they felt a little awkward calling them Pete and Mrs. Simmons. I don't know who started it, but the tradition was begun. Even at home, I sometimes referred to them as Pete and Gladys, especially when my girlfriends were visiting or spending the night.

Boy Scouts: Troop 104

There have been countless boys in the Broken Arrow community who have evolved into adulthood armed with survival skills along with stories and memories of Pete's leadership during scout meetings and camping experiences. A few of these were my classmates, which made them special to me. David Hartman and I have known each other since we were in the nursery at First Methodist Church, so I can testify Pete had his hands full with this teenager. He developed into a fine young man with good ethics and morals and became a real estate appraiser. We communicated recently when he asked me about Daddy's military experience. When I asked him to contribute his scouting stories, he had this to say about Pete's influence on him:

Pete Simmons was like a surrogate father figure most boys encounter while growing up, not unlike a Little League coach or a Sunday school teacher or a public education teacher. These are the kinds of people that your parents hand you over to for additional education and experience.

As a scoutmaster, Pete was tough, a taskmaster, but looking back, he had to really care to endure year after year of volunteer time that he could have otherwise have used for his own recreation or family time. I think that maybe his higher calling was tempered by his need to be in the spotlight, to have an audience, because he was always doing something outrageous with his scouts.

What would now be considered not to be politically correct, Pete would perform his famous cigarette tricks with a lighted cigarette, flipping them in the air and catching the correct end between his lips. Another would be to fill a cup with smoke and pour it into an awaiting cup. I vaguely recall there were more because it would not be like Pete to have only two.

One thing we all knew as scouts was Pete had been in combat as a Marine. Part of his uniform at scout meetings, campouts and hikes was an army green campaign hat, the kind we associate with WWII and a Marine Drill Instructor. Being too young to have a larger sense of where he fought, I don't believe he ever talked about too many war details. I learned from his daughter Jan that his war activity was the south Pacific, namely Guadalcanal.

He did give us the reason he was a scoutmaster. On the troop train home, after the war, they had an officer on board that gave them a talk on re-integration into civilian life. He told the soldiers to get involved in civic matters. It did not matter what, just get involved, whether it be church, school or politics. Obviously, Pete chose scouting and he remained true to the cause.

The scouts had a summer camp location in the Cookson Hills in northeastern Oklahoma, our Troop 14 always attended. The camps were spread out, with troops from various towns occupying their own camps. The grounds we hiked were hilly and wooded. The water in the bottom land creek was clear and good for water hiking and shallow swimming. The shallow gravel bottomed creek would have been difficult to drown in, even in the worst condition. A friend and I snuck off for a swim, a forbidden activity. When Pete found out, he went ballistic and threatened to call our parents to come retrieve us. He became more and more emotional and ended up crying in front of us out of frustration. Our parents had entrusted Pete to take care of their kids and he took the mission seriously, just like a dedicated Marine would.

Looking back, I see now that Pete was a small town attorney. Any time away from his practice was time lost for income production. With a wife and three kids to support, this was no small matter. Of course, to us scouts, we were not conscious of the time he devoted to us. For awhile, Pete and his family lived off Main Street in Broken Arrow, in an apartment behind his office, I believe. Most likely it wasn't ideal, not like having a house and a yard to play in. I think back on the time from war's end to when he was my scoutmaster, say, to the late 1950's. In that time he had to attend and complete law school and get a practice up and running. He had a full plate, to be sure. I look back on that now with great admiration. It had to have been difficult, not only for Pete but also for Frances, his wife.

Pete danced to his own drummer. In 1950's Broken Arrow, the beetle Volkswagen was a striking oddity, very exotic. It was small and odd looking and underpowered. You saw them only rarely, but of course they became iconic and they were everywhere. Well, Pete did not buy a VW, he bought a Renault Dauphin. Similar in size to the VW, it was a pretty little car with a French design. Their advertisements featured the 2-tone horn. You'd honk the horn (beep,beep), flip a switch and it would beep, beep to a different note. Pete used that to the max, beeping the horn in the same manner as on TV and all us scouts would squeal with delight.

There was a moderately steep hill on 71st, west of Sheridan Road. Pete would always coast down it, gathering speed, again delighting the scouts riding with him. The sensation of silent speed was thrilling at the time. I doubt we ever topped 60mph at the bottom of the hill. It was just something my parents never did, and it seemed so exciting at the time.

Donnie Anderson was David's partner in crime. Donnie worked for many years with Boeing and now works at Tinker Air Force Base. This is his story:

Pete Simmons and Troop 104

I have been told by many that I was pretty wild as kids go and during this period my dad Andy was trying his best to keep me under control. Andy was a scout master in Arkansas and also an Eagle Scout and active participant supporting different troops for years.

We were members of the Methodist Church in Broken Arrow, OK and my dad wanted me to join the Boy Scouts of America. I had already completed my tenure as a Cub Scout and Webelos which means: 'We'll be Loyal Scouts.' The next step of this progression in the boy scouts is to proceed through the different ranks until you reached Eagle. However, at this point in my life, I was more interested in girls, motorcycles and cars than building camp fires!

One Sunday after church, Mr. Simmons introduced himself as the Scout Master of Troop 104 and asked me to join. He said he discussed it with my dad who volunteered to help out with Mr. McCarty. Mr. Simmons went on to explain how important it would be to be a part of something good and that the things I would learn would stay with me for a lifetime. From an attorney's standpoint: "How to Stay out of Trouble!" He ended with, 'Just call me Pete.'

I agreed out of respect for my dad more than anything else. However, later on I was glad that I did, since I learned that everything he said was true. I was sworn in with several other new recruits at the next scout meeting. The ceremony was conducted at Camp Russell, followed by an overnight campout which was a great success. I met all of the other scouts in the troop and I learned we had to go through initiation from the older scouts. _Wait a minute! There had been no mention of initiations until that moment!_

Larry Keene and Chris Simmons stepped up to explain I had to be tested to see if I was scout material and good enough to be in the troop. The first test was to catch a snipe, an animal that only moves at night. I did not even know what one looked like. I was taken to a very dark area of the camp to hold this carbide light that gave out a very dim light. I was instructed to hold the bag open while beating on a log and the other boys would make a big circle to run the snipe toward my direction. According to the guys, the snipe would be attracted to the flickering light and the beating sound. My job was to quickly close the bag after the snipe ran in before he got away. A long period of time had passed before they returned. Of course they had a bigger laugh from the initiation than the new scouts.

The older scouts had other initiation stunts for us. After being blindfolded and pushed into briars into a creek, Pete came to our rescue. Pete pulled me out of the water and told the guys 'things are getting out of hand'. I was soaked but my clothes dried out at the campfire. As for me: _'Yea, I am now officially a Boy Scout of Troop 104!'_

Pete provided a field trip to the Tulsa County Court House to illustrate that it was not a good place to go unless you worked there. He received permission from a judge for us observe a few 'real court cases' in action. A deputy took us for a tour of the jail. This was a real eye-opener for young scouts!

We went on numerous hikes and overnight campouts to Camp Russell, Lake Tenkiller and many times to Para-

dise Cove at Sequoyah State Park and one trip to Ozark Arkansas. Pete, Mr. McCarty and my dad would help us work toward our merit badges and ratings and learn new things. One time Pete decided he wanted everyone to learn how to shoot rifles having a competition shoot at the end. In addition, he gave three cash prizes to the best marksmen. He brought two 22 caliber training rifles that looked like the M1 Rifles. To illustrate how times have changed since then. The contest was held at the Old First Methodist Church on the East Side where there was a dirt berm that we shot toward. First place was a dollar bill, second place was a fifty cent piece and third place was a quarter. I out shot everyone in the troop, was awarded a dollar bill and Pete said, 'You're a natural Donnie, I could make a marine sniper out of you!'

Although I was working at the time, Pete, my dad, and Mrs. McCarty took some of the members of Troop 104 to Philmont Scout Ranch. The highlight of our year were trips to Camp Garland close to home.

The first time I went to Camp Garland, Pete went over the camp rules and informed us that the Girl Scout Camp was just down the river from our camp. Furthermore, he said pretty loud; "I don't want any of you guys going near the Girl Scout Camp and under no circumstances are you to go down there!"

We promptly replied, "Yes Sir!" We were good for two days following all the rules. Then on the third day, one of the guys suggested we should sneak down to see what the girls are doing, 'just go have a look see because that should not hurt anything'. Wouldn't you know the scout that did not go with us check out the girls told Pete! We couldn't figure out at the time why he was smiling during this repri-

mand. Although we tested his patience many times, he was a good man and a really good Scoutmaster. We did not realize it at the time but these were some of the best times of our lives when life was simpler and a whole lot more fun!

By Donnie Anderson, Troop 104   February 2, 2015

The final story is by Raymond Sturm, another classmate who coincidentally became an attorney. He lives in Austin, Texas.

Recollections of Pete Simmons

We had several camping trips when Pete was our Scoutmaster. Most of these were at Camp Russell Scout Camp south of BA. Once when we went to Mohawk Park it rained HARD and flooded our campground during the night. There was a very severe thunderstorm and it is a miracle someone did not get struck by lightning. Everything we had, and I mean everything, got soaked. But we still had a great time.

Everyone pitched in and I remember drying our sleeping bags and clothes by draping them over our tents the next morning. If the weather had been beautiful, I am sure I would not have remembered this camping trip. But since we had to face a little adversity and overcome it, made it more memorable. We were so brave!!

Another thing I remember about Pete was when he taught us how to do a compass hike at night with just a flashlight and our compasses. Today they call it something similar to "orienteering." That was a lot of fun, and it taught us that we could rely on the compass to find our way even in the dark.

We had some great times and our meetings were al-

ways learning experiences. Pete always had something up his sleeve to keep the meetings interesting.

Daddy was scout master for several years. There were many other young Broken Arrow boys who were in his troop before and after these boys. He had nicknames for a few. I remember he called Barry Ray "Bear Track" When he asked Barry his name, he thought that was Barry's reply. Richard Cannon may have gotten his nickname "Boom Boom" that way as well.

In Season and Out

Pete seemed to always be in public speaking and teaching mode as he continued to be available to speak on Veteran's Day, Law Day in classrooms for his daughter, Barbara and granddaughters. I video taped a talk he gave about the court system to a Civics class at Childers Middle School for his granddaughter, Mollie when he was seventy-five years old.

He felt like it was vitally important for people of all ages to understand American history, our Constitution, how our government system works and to know our rights as Americans. He always volunteered in the community in which he lived and encouraged others to be involved.

Philmont Scout Ranch: Pete and other Scoutmasters from across the country meet to learn new camping and scouting skills.

Chapter 16
REST FOR THE WEARY
- VACATION TIME FINALLY

Our dad had a love for adventure and travel, perhaps a yearning from his railroad hopping days. Because he was busy building his law practice from the early- to mid-fifties and had young children, he kept most of our outings centered around visiting family, the farthest being Hugo, Oklahoma, to see our Great Grandmother Neighbors.

The earliest ventures I recall us making in Oklahoma are Beavers Bend State Park near Broken Bow and Idabel, Robbers' Cave State Park near Wilburton, and the Great Salt Plains in the western part of the state. Pete's theory was "see your own state first".

Chris, Barbara and Jan at Robber's Cave State Park, August 1956.

As we grew older, the real vacations began. Since our dad was the Boy Scout Master at our church, we traveled to Philmont Scout Ranch, near Cimarron, New Mexico during the summer of 1957. We pitched our family tent among the others in a long row. They had a variety of family activities throughout the week, from woodburning to belt-making for family members while the scouts worked on badges and learned new skills. They were well-organized activities and grouped by age and gender. It was enjoyable as well as educational.

Archery Practice at Philmont Scout Ranch: Chris shown third from left.

Alaska, the Last Frontier

The most adventuresome and fabulous vacation a child and the whole family could only dream about came true for us in

1959. Our dad had corresponded with a law firm whose legal secretary was Pauline Showman Unruh, Paul and Loyd Showman's sister. After communicating back and forth for a while, he made a plan.

Our first step was to go by and visit with Jack Murray's Plymouth dealership on Kenosha in Broken Arrow. Mother and Daddy chose a 1959 white Plymouth station wagon for the trip. Not all cars were equipped with air conditioning as standard options during those days. Daddy decided the weather would be mild enough driving through Canada and Alaska in June, so we would not need air conditioning.

We went to Warehouse Market on Main Street as a family and stocked up on groceries to avoid eating in restaurants along the way. As soon as school had ended for the semester, we headed "North to Alaska." Daddy had mapped out the trip to see other sights along the way. We drove through Wyoming and Montana into Canada. We missed the largest rodeo in the nation in Cheyenne by a few days, but did see the capital. As was our custom, we stopped along the way to attend church. We could always find a Methodist Church wherever we went. We attended the Methodist Church in Riverton, Wyoming.

From Wyoming we traveled through Montana. Then we traveled into Canada. We had been warned we would not be able to take raw food such as bacon across the border into Canada. We had not eaten up all our bacon from previous mornings of camping along the way, so Daddy made a plan to camp right before we crossed the border and cook it up that next morning. That is still one of my fondest memories of the whole trip. How peaceful it was to wake up next to the sound of a serene waterfall and smell of slabs of thick bacon frying in a cast iron skillet over an open fire as we emerged one by one from Daddy's old Marine tent. It was as picturesque as one could only imagine in magazines. As it turned out, when we crossed the border, the agent did not inspect our car or even ask us about carrying raw pork.

Jan, Chris and Pete posing in front of their new 1959 Plymouth station wagon Pete bought specifically to drive to Alaska that summer by way of the old Alcan Highway.

Daddy did most of the driving, but Mother did her fair share while Daddy rested. One adventure we had was driving through the area of Calgary, Alberta. When we stopped for gas, the attendant told us about a young man from his hometown who had escaped from an insane asylum in the region. He had killed several members of his immediate family. Leaving the station, we kept the radio tuned for the latest reports. The Royal Mounted Police had narrowed down the area in which he had last been seen. They were strategically placed to form a dragnet to surround him in the area. It was exactly the region through which we were driving. Stern warnings were announced on the radio to not stop for any hitchhikers or strangers. Mother assured Daddy she could handle the drive through the area, so he stretched out in the back of the station wagon to sleep for an hour or so. The sky full of stars was beautiful as we traveled through the mountains of Canada during the night. But as the night got darker, it became more suspenseful. Chris sat in the front seat to keep a watch out with Mother. I could hardly sleep for the excitement of it.

All of sudden coming down a long stretch of straight high-way from a rather tall hill, there appeared to be a man standing in the middle of the road. The closer we got we could see him waving his arms. The words echoed in Mother's head: "Do not stop for anyone!" But the closer she got, the more she realized he was not moving from his position in the road. He waved his arms even more, flailing them wildly! As if mesmerized by his figure in a trance, Mother was staring as she quickly approached this maniac on the highway! She screamed, "Wake up, Pete!" About that time as Daddy scrambled to see the action, he yelled at her to not run over him. The tall dark figure barely jumped out of the way! The Mounted Police officer narrowly escaped death as Mother came to a screeching halt. After he recovered from the shock, the Mounty and another officer whom we had not detected earlier appeared from the side of the road. They shined flashlights all through the car. When finished, tipping

Traveling across a temporary suspension bridge in Canada because the highway was washed out.

his hat the officer reminded us to "not stop for any hitchhikers or strangers along the way." Later on that night the Canadian Mounted Police apprehended their man so all was well. By that time we were past that area.

We had other fun adventures from Calgary, Alberta to White-horse, Yukon but not quite as exciting as Calgary. Along the way we saw old deserted mining towns, tall mountains and other beautiful forestry, but our next 'more than just an every day event' was crossing a railroad bridge by car. They had closed part of the highway for construction but converted a railroad bridge into a temporary suspension bridge to make a way for cars to cross a ravine by traveling from one side of it to the other. We crossed it seemingly inch by inch trying not to look down. Some of us family members would rather have taken a different route through those mountains instead of taking the chance, but it was the only direct route. Besides, Pete was always game for anything risky.

Other things we saw were giant heads of cabbage growing in farming fields of Palmer, Alaska. It had been raining and we took a picture of a rainbow up against a mountain that actually showed up on the film. Another unique experience was standing on the bank of the bay in Seward where Will Rogers and Wiley Post took off in their plane for the last time before dying in a crash at Point Barrow, Alaska. We enjoyed the sights of Fairbanks and Anchorage where we saw rows and rows of saloons. When the prospectors came in the late 1800's to mine for gold, they made a law there had to be a church built for every saloon. So churches were scattered throughout the town. I remember it snowed about one hundred miles outside of Anchorage, so we stopped the car to have a snowball fight. It ended quickly as most of the snow had melted, and the puddles attracted mosquitoes in the puddles. So back in the car we went.

Once we arrived in Anchorage, there were many things to

visit. Among the sightseeing attractions was a museum that may have been owned and operated by a taxidermist. Its display was a hunter's paradise of trophies as wild animals, indigenous to that part of our country were mounted and positioned to appear as if in their natural environment.

The museum was not in itself unusual as they offered tours like many other animal exhibits in museums do. But a unique thing about this museum was the fur store located in the back of the building before exiting. It was quite a marketing strategy. There were many beautiful fur coats on racks and mannequins ranging from mink to fox furs including children's sizes. Anyone who remembers watching the Bess Myerson Show when she came on stage in a full-length mink coat during the early days of television could possibly visualize the two little Simmons girls in a dreamland of luxury and softness of fur. I remember we squealed and begged, "Daddy please buy us fur coats!" How could this dad who always wanted to lavish his children with nice things refuse? We left the store loaded with shopping bags of rabbit parkas with hoods decoratively edged with wolf fur along with a pair of mukluks, boots for Chris made of seal and walrus. The parkas were not only practical but especially durable enough we wore them to school that following winter. I still have my parka and recently showed it to my granddaughter, Audrey

Audrey Grace Hopkins posing in her grandmother's parka.

Grace Hopkins. It fits her well, although I was twelve, and she is only eight years old.

Our Alaskan venture would not have been complete without Daddy giving us all nicknames: Fairbanks Fran, Ketchikan Chris, Juneau Jan and Point Barrow Barb. We finished our vacation that summer by coming down the Pacific coast through Washington and Oregon into California. While we were in the Los Angeles area we visited with friends our folks knew during the war, went to a Dodgers baseball game and had an adventure at Disneyland, which had newly opened the year before in 1958. The rest of our travels took us through the Grand Canyon in Arizona, then New Mexico and home. The whole month of June, 1959, was quite an adventure for a Simmons family summer vacation!

Hola, Mexico, 1963!

Daddy took us southwest the summer of 1963, perhaps with visions of sombreros and ponchos as souvenirs in mind. He reminded us our English word 'souvenir' originated from a French word which means 'to remember.' By now we had a 1963 Ford Fairlane station wagon. We traveled this time across New Mexico, then south through Phoenix and Tucson, Arizona crossing the United States border at Nogales into Sonora. There was an obvious difference between the roads in our country and Mexico.

We traveled though the beautiful countryside seeing a different kind of mountain range than those in Canada and Alaska. Enjoying mild early summer weather, we saw in the far distance a peach grove along the highway. As we came closer, we could see what we thought was a worker in the grove, but soon realized it was a man just picking fruit from one of the peach trees. Seeing us, he emerged from the peach grove and walked toward the road. By the time we approached him, he was standing beside the road. Pockets bulging with freshly-picked peaches and holding a few peaches in his hands, this traveler managed to raise a thumb to hitch a ride. Slowly and cautiously passing by on the left side of the road, Daddy had only seconds to decide if this man looked harmless enough to offer a ride. Most people would not have even considered giving a stranger a ride, but not Pete! He had been a "bum" once himself and had hitched many rides. The stranger gave a little nod, a smile and cast a glance our way. With that, Daddy pulled over to the side of the road. I'm sure at this point Mother was reprimanding with words of caution, safety and whatever else she could think to say to deter this next action. But the warnings went by the wayside. In the next few moments, we were switching seats around with Mother moving to the back seat, leaving the men on the front bench seat. In no time at all, we felt he was safe.

Our New Amigo

We quickly had a new friend in Raoul as we were immersed in a Spanish lesson. Daddy and Chris had taken Spanish in school, but Raoul's local dialect and colloquialisms were somewhat different than the way they had learned. The three in the front seat were more interactive than the girls. They discovered quickly if they wanted to learn a new word in Spanish, they just pointed at the object and ask, "Cómo se dice?" which translated is 'How do you say …'? Raoul would quickly supply us with the Spanish word. Having just graduated from high school and finishing his Spanish course with Mrs. Genevieve Allen, Chris was enjoying this practical use of his vocabulary. Seeing a cow in the pasture Chris proudly pointed and provided the word "Vaca."

Raoul nodded and added with a pointed finger, "Si, Vaca Pinta." Needing more interpretation, Chris looked to Daddy for assistance.

Daddy completed the thought with "Pinto Cow" as he laughed, teaching Raoul a new word in English with his response: "Spotted cow, a Holstein."

Raoul cautiously repeated, "Holstein. Ah…. Holstein." The trip continued with our learning and using words like that as we snacked on stolen peaches.

During this venture we had many lessons within lessons and have many stories within our stories to tell. We traveled on to the south and then back east stopping in Cananea, one of the largest towns in the area. We noticed they had a Ford dealership in town and a restaurant with hotel. It was about lunch time so we decided to eat. Entering the establishment which was actually not much bigger than a small café, only two other people were there at a table in the corner. We found a table large enough in the middle of the room. Raoul found a table on the other side of the room, but Daddy motioned for him to sit with us. He may have been a down-and-outer but not as long as he was with us.

Daddy began talking to the other two diners who were American engineers doing work in the area. Their presence was convenient because they assisted us by reading the menu. They provided us with the names of the entrées Daddy did not know. One engineer was stumped on one dinner selection as he contemplated and tried to retrieve it from his memory. He said, "I don't remember what it is in Spanish, but I know the words in French," as he provided the phrase in French. Daddy laughed as he announced, "Liver and onions." All the adults in the room had a great laugh! That later became one of Daddy's favorite stories as he was able to teach an object lesson about how important it is to learn to speak different languages.

Once we had our meal, we said our goodbyes and were on our way once again with our new friend, Raoul. The further away from town we traveled, the less green the grass became and the more desolate the countryside. We learned that mileage was figured by how many cattle crossings one had passed. About thirty minutes out of town we approached an area with a downhill slope. We saw the typical yellow warning signs containing words like "Vada" and "Despasio" on them. Although this time Pete knew the words, in his typical humorous fashion, he chose to ignore them, as he shrugged his shoulders and pretended not to understand. He actually sped up the car to reiterate and exaggerate his feigned ignorance of the signs' meanings. Raoul's demeanor however, expressed immediate concern as he waved his hands and said, "No, despasio, despasio! Vada!" It was too late for Daddy to avoid the consequences of his joke. The yellow warning signs for "slow" and "dip" went unheeded as our station wagon bounced hard. As the road dipped in a low spot, we heard a loud noise which was the broken gas tank bracket dragging on the road. We were fortunate the gas tank did not explode.

Raoul jumped out of the car and motioned for all of us to run for safety. He pulled off his belt and climbed under the car to try to tie it back up to no avail. Daddy told him to not even try. Thankfully after a short time a truck came down the road that had emptied their load of crushed lime. Daddy decided the three men should stay with the car and he sent Mother, Barbara and me into town to the Ford Motor Company to send a wrecker out for our Ford Fairlane.

Three Mexican men sat in the front as we climbed into the back of the truck. We had wrap-around skirts on with shorts underneath. The lime dust left from the truck's load became unbearable, swirling around getting into our eyes, so we resorted to pulling our skirts up over our faces. We had to endure the laughter of the men but we made it into town. We were unloaded on Main Street right in front of the Ford Motor Company. We were glad it was not Main Street of Broken Arrow! As soon as Mother had the wrecker sent out to pull the car in, we headed toward the hotel and restaurant to clean up.

Once the car was repaired the next day, we were on our way back to New Mexico again. Raoul had told Pete his goal was to come to America for freedom and a better quality of life. As we approached the United States border, he said he wanted to be a "Wet Back." We parted at the border and wished him well. It was quite an adventure, and we never forgot Raoul.

New York, 1964

Vacationing to far-away and interesting or unusual locations was not always a yearly event for the Simmons family. However, the following year was a Presidential election so our trip in 1964 was focused on going to the National Democratic Convention in Atlantic City, New Jersey. The World's Fair was also being held in the United States that year in New York City. The two cities were in geographical proximity, so Daddy planned for us to do both activities in a reasonable amount of time.

We had borrowed Uncle Earl's pop-up camper and used it along the way. The camper could be used in case we were in between cities or if there were no available rooms in motels along the way. There were smaller towns in New York state enroute to New York City. I remember arriving in one town late at night. As it would happen, there were no motel rooms available. However, there was what appeared to be a park along side the road. So Daddy decided to stop and pop up the camper. He was too tired to travel any further. In the morning, we awoke to the noise of city traffic bustling around us. We had literally 'pitched our tent' in the city park. We gathered up our blankets, Daddy racked down the camper, and we were on our way again. It felt like we were country folks on our way to the big city for the first time.

World's Fair

We had contemplated staying at a bed and breakfast with a casual atmosphere as opposed to a regular hotel, but as we arrived in New York City, it was more difficult than we anticipated getting a place to stay because of so many World's Fair visitors. At one of our stops, it was suggested we stay in the home of people who were willing to rent out a portion of their home for the World's Fair. A couple who lived in Flushing, New York was recommended to us and we headed that direction. The couple was very nice and we enjoyed our time while we stayed there. We had a wonderful time visiting the exhibits from the different countries during the World's Fair and had ample time to see some of the sights in New York City as well. Daddy enjoyed seeing New York City for the first time as much as we did.

One of the most humorous things we remembered from the trip related to the Flushing couple. By this time we were in the habit of teasing our parents with their nicknames of Pete and Gladys. It may have sounded a little disrespectful to our parents but they did not seem to mind it.

That Christmas and in subsequent years we received nice Christmas cards from our friends with whom we stayed in Flushing. It was addressed to 'Pete and Gladys' Simmons. I don't suppose Mother corrected them in the error. We found it to be amusing each year when their Christmas card arrived.

Ticket to National Democratic Convention

National Democratic Convention, 1964

From New York we headed south to Philadelphia and visited historical sights there. We continued on to Atlantic City, New Jersey. This time we had made reservations for a hotel to attend the National Democratic Convention. Daddy was a delegate at the convention so he had planned this part of the vacation well in advance.

We had another unexpected adventure with the pop-up camper. This time it was not just a small town. We were right downtown Atlantic City. Unbeknownst to us some of the streets were one-way leading directly to the boardwalk. The street on which we ended up took us straight to the hotel close to where the convention center was. It was an old and regal hotel. As we arrived, Daddy realized there was no street to turn left or right and no room for us to make a U-turn because the camper and station wagon were too long.

Usually most situations were ones Pete could laugh about, but not this one. Being a delegate to a national convention was too closely associated with his profession. He usually did not care about appearances, but this time he did. He did not want to appear like a 'country bumpkin' going to town for the first time. He and Chris had the humiliating job of getting the camper turned around but we were right directly in front of the entrance of the hotel. The doorman was embarrassed and without having direct eye contact, was motioning with his white-gloved hands for us to "remove ourselves immediately from the premises." They had no alternative other than getting the back tire in a bouncing position to bounce each corner of the camper around slowly and laboriously. Mother had to turn the wheel as we are taught in drivers' education and slowly do a turn-about in the middle of the city street. It was finally accomplished. I did my part as a teenager. I hid behind a newspaper in the back seat. Once we were removed from that situation we found a parking garage further away in another area. We got checked into the hotel and settled in. From that point on it was more enjoyable.

During the time we were there, we saw many of our United States Senators and Congressmen. It was really an exciting time at Convention Hall to see many of the people we only heard about from the news or saw them reporting the news, like Walter Cronkite. Daddy discreetly pointed out Senators and Congressmen arriving. Senator Pierre Salinger is one the main ones we saw. He served as a White House Press Secretary for both John Fitzgerald Kennedy and Lyndon Baines Johnson. Daddy wanted us to know who the leaders of our Nation were. Just being in Convention Hall was unique because it is the same building in which the Miss America pageants had always been held.

Attending a national political convention is an event every citizen should experience at least once. For the politically-minded, it could likely be attended more often. Part of the time family members of delegates were allowed to go down on the main floor, but not during voting times toward the end of the week. Once when we were allowed on the main floor, Daddy introduced us to our Oklahoma Congressman and Speaker of the House, Carl

Albert. He was from Bugtussle, Oklahoma. That was one of the highlights of our trip to Atlantic City. What a memory!

A Small Scuffle

Anytime there are huge political events, there are people gathered to protest different causes. We saw a group of hippie-like people protesting the war in Viet Nam. It was not impressive to us because they appeared not to have bathed in several days. There was a group of Nazi protestors who we girls missed seeing because of shopping on the boardwalk. But the newspaper did not miss the event as it was published in an Atlantic City newspaper the next day.

There was an odd assortment of several groups of protesters on the boardwalk near Convention Hall. A group of Mississippi Freedom Democrats had been squatting on their site since midnight of the previous day. The trouble began when the American Nazi party came too close to the group who were already occupying their spot without discord. The Nazi group was met by state policemen and loaded into a paddy wagon.

The newspaper stated the melee began when "a former marine punched one of the pickets who was carrying an 'LBJ the Traitor' placard." As it happened, Pete and Chris were on the boardwalk at that very moment. They witnessed this whole event. I was relieved to know Daddy was not the marine who hit the protester. They were certainly excited when they told us the story. Another picketer was punched by a young man whose family had been executed in Nazi Germany. His sentence was suspended.

Lyndon Banes Johnson, LBJ, was the Democratic nominee that summer and was elected United States President in November. We learned a lot from our experiences, especially ones that become a part of American history. It was always nice to be home again to normal activities, though.

Daddy never lacked a desire to seek out adventurous vacations. That enjoyment for travel, especially visiting historical sites, was passed on to his children.

Paul E. 'Pete' Simmons was nominated and accepted by acclamation as new mayor of Broken Arrow, Oklahoma on May 2, 1966.

Chapter 17
HOMETOWN POLITICS

Paul E. "Pete" Simmons felt comfortable in city government. He had experience as Municipal City Judge in the early 1950s. He unsuccessfully ran for state representative. He always had a 'never give up' attitude. He also ran but was defeated in a school board election. In the mid-1960's he ran a successful campaign for Broken Arrow City Councilman. A quarter-page advertisement appeared in The Broken Arrow Ledger during the campaign. It was paid for by contributions from members of the Wesley Class of the First Methodist Church. He won the election and began his first term as councilman in 1964.

Prohibition and Home Brew

In 1964 we moved to the third house we called home in Broken Arrow as a family. Crockett's farm had become a housing addition and all of us "horse-riding" families had to find new places to board our horses. Our new home, 2401 S. Elm Place had a few acres to keep our horses. It was just south of 91st Street (Washington). Elm Place continued

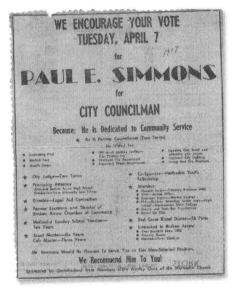

Ad for Broken Arrow City Councilman
• Courtesy of Broken Arrow Ledger

to have new traffic traveling it daily. After Daddy won the election for City Council, our property had to be annexed into Broken Arrow's city limits because 91st Street was the border and at the edge of what 'town' was in 1964.

One weekend Chris was home from college. I am unsure how the conversation actually started, but Chris and Daddy were talking about prohibition and how Oklahoma state laws were somewhat different than other states. One thing lead to another and before long they decided to make some home brew. It was perfectly legal if it was made for home consumption and not to market or sell. Daddy shifted into teaching mode and set up a home economics class with ingredients, such as barley, hops, water and yeast along with pop bottles and corks as containers. They obtained some old-fashioned crocks and mixed up their concoction. The fermentation was probably the longest part of the process. Once finished, they bottled it. Daddy stored their finished product in the garage. They did not quite get the color right. Instead of a beautiful champagne color it was almost bright orange. They were probably more concerned with the taste than looks of their recipe.

Two carpenters came to the house to do some repairs for Daddy a few days after he and Chris completed their home brew project. Daddy left the garage door open for them if they needed electricity. They saw a chain saw and some other power tools. When Daddy came home from the office he noticed the garage door was still open and his chain saw and tools were gone. He noticed his special recipe of home brew was nowhere in sight. None of our family members had seen the men or anything unusual. Thanks to an observant eye by a neighbor, Audra Denny, she was able to identify the make and model of their car. The theft was reported to the police.

Monday evenings were City Council meetings so Daddy ate a quick supper and headed toward city hall. He gave Mother strict instructions what to do if the men returned. Daddy had not yet paid the men for the job they had completed. As he suspected they would do, the men came back to collect their wages. They showed up at the front door and rang the doorbell. Barbara and I were home with Mother. It was obvious the men had stolen and consumed all of Daddy and Chris' home brew. They both had poor equilibrium and could barely stand up. As instructed Mother told them she had a shotgun behind the door and if they did not bring back the chain saw, tools and beer immediately she was going to shoot them. They apologized with "Yes ma'am. We'll be right back. But we're sorry we can not bring back that orange pop. We drank it all."

She said "Mr. Simmons is really mad you stole his tools, but he's especially mad you stole his home brew." Within minutes they were back and left the stolen items on the porch.

The police report was published in the Broken Arrow Ledger. It stated, "There was a robbery at City Councilman Paul Simmons' home yesterday. There were some power tools stolen along with a beverage of homemade variety."

Paul E. Simmons served as Mayor from 1966 to 1967

Mayor of Broken Arrow

There is a great deal of responsibility in managing the affairs of a city or town. There are difficult decisions to be made at times, but there are also everyday activities that are in need of attention. The Mayor and city councilmen have many more common items on their weekly agenda than large ones. Johnnie Parks provided me with Broken Arrow City Council minutes from 1965 through 1967 to be included in Daddy's story. According to city council minutes in January, 1965 Loren Gall was Broken Arrow's Mayor, Jim Jackson was Vice-Mayor and councilmen were Charlie Vaughn, Clyde Cline and Paul Simmons. During the next term, May, 1965, Jim Jackson was Mayor and Fred Gesin was Vice-Mayor. Some of those everyday activities were often humorous:

A lady appeared before the council protesting the dogs running loose. Motion by Mr. Simmons and seconded by Mr. Cline to instruct the city attorney to draw up an ordinance raising the dog license fees to $2.00 on a male or spayed female and $3.00 on a female. Motion carried.

For his first term as Mayor, Pete was nominated in this way on May 2, 1966:

Motion by Mr. [Barney] Cheek, seconded by Mr. [James] Newcomb to nominate Paul Simmons as Mayor. Motion by Mr. Cheek, seconded by Mr. Newcomb that nominations cease and Mr. Simmons be elected by acclamation. Motion carried.

During Mayor Simmons' term of office he accomplished several 'firsts' in Broken Arrow's progress.

'This Is the Mayor . . .'

This will be the scene Monday morning as Mayor James Hewgley of Tulsa (left) talks with Mayor Paul Simmons of Broken Arrow to officially open extended area service dialing between the two cities.

Subscribers in both cities simply dial numbers listed in directories. No tolls will be charged. Broken Arrow tolls will remain on calls from and to three Tulsa area exchanges: Circle 5 (Sand Springs), ATlantic 5 (Sperry), and CRestview 2 (Owasso).

Actually, all phones will be linked on Sunday, ahead of the official opening. The switch has been costly to both Southwestern Bell Telephone Co., of Tulsa, and General Telephone Co., of Broken Arrow.

There will be no additional cost to Tulsa users, but the Broken Arrow business rate for a single line has been increased from $11.50 to $16.25 monthly and single line residential service from $6.40 to $7.66, with increases for other types of service as well.

The Tulsa Tribune
TULSA, OKLA., SATURDAY, FEBRUARY 4, 1967   PAGE 13

This is the Mayor... Mayor Hewgley initiates telephone service from Broken Arrow to Tulsa without long distance charges
• Used by permission The Tulsa Tribune

"Operator, Please Connect Me"

As late as the 1960's, Broken Arrowans were assessed toll charges to make telephone calls to Tulsa. Today with mobile and cell phones, we do not remember phone numbers as we once did. Older residents from that time remember Pioneer 8 which was originally assigned to Broken Arrow as the city's prefix and Pilgrim 6 for Bixby's. Tulsa had zones or exchanges that prefixes were also used as well as those assigned to surrounding towns.

During Daddy's mayoral term of office, steps were taken to

215

initiate telephone lines that would allow Broken Arrow citizens to access direct calling to Tulsa. Mayor James Hewgley from Tulsa and Mayor Paul E. Simmons from Broken Arrow were pleased to officially announce Monday, February 6, 1967, as the date set for the elimination of long distance charges. An article appeared in The Tulsa Tribune on Saturday, February 4, 1967 that was captioned:

'This is the Mayor...'

This will be the scene Monday morning as Mayor James Hewgley of Tulsa (left) talks with Mayor Paul Simmons of Broken Arrow to officially open extended area service dialing between the two cities.

Subscribers in both cities simply dial numbers listed in directories. No tolls will be charged. Broken Arrow tolls will remain on calls from and to three Tulsa area exchanges: Circle 6 (Sand Springs), Atlantic 8 (Sperry), and Crestview 2 Owasso).

Actually, all phones will be linked on Sunday, ahead of the official opening. The switch has been costly to both Southwestern Bell Telephone Co., of Tulsa, and General Telephone Co., of Broken Arrow.

There will be no additional cost to Tulsa users, but the Broken Arrow business rate for a single line has been increased from $11.50 to $16.25 monthly and single line residential service from $6.40 to $7.60, with increases for other types of service as well.

Broken Arrow Deserves Better Water

I remember him traveling to Atlanta and other areas to inspect and pursue better water treatment possibilities for our city water. He initiated the Verdigris Water Treatment Plant. The new plant was dedicated on April 21, 1967.

Broken Arrow old water tower seen above the City Hall and jail, next to the fire department and library on Dallas Street.
• Broken Arrow Historical Museum

Broken Arrow Expressway

I recall my friend Sue Samuel Lenard's mother, Barbara Samuel, reminding me a few years ago that 'Pete was the only one in favor of building four and six-lanes for the Broken Arrow Expressway in planning for future growth' probably because of the cost. She told me comments were made such as "that expressway will never have the traffic going to Tulsa that the regular streets will have", thus rejecting his request and campaign for it.

Another street discussed to possibly four-lane was Elm Place. One of the City

The Broken Arrow Expressway breaks new ground, ca. 1964..

217

Councilman said Broken Arrowans do not want Elm to become another busy street like Memorial in Tulsa. Again, comments were made expressing the fact Elm would never take the place of Main Street. It would have ultimately saved Broken Arrow millions of dollars to have accepted the proposal during that time especially when traffic was much lighter. Mayor Paul (Pete) Simmons was always a visionary.

Paying Honor

Daddy had high regard for Bill Secrest as Broken Arrow City Manager. He felt that he performed his duties in an exceptionally fine manner. At one council meeting he suggested the Council consider raises for the legal department which were approved. It was also brought out that Mr. F.A. Petrik had served the Council for 30 years and was deserving of an increase in salary.

On area planning he stressed the need to obtain Federal Grants. He urged the Council and others to become actively concerned with this planning program for the best interest in the future growth and needs of Broken Arrow.

My Hometown Disappointed Me

Pete ran for Mayor of Broken Arrow for a second term and was defeated. His opponent was a young man who had only graduated from Broken Arrow a few years earlier. He was inexperienced and many of the townspeople did not really take this campaign seriously. As a result, some the people did not vote in that election. Those who supported this young man showed up and voted. Daddy understood that when one is in politics, one cannot always please everyone. He still believed it was a right and a privilege to express one's opinion and support by voting for one or the other candidate.

When Daddy lost the election by only a few votes, people were surprised and admitted to him they had no doubts that he would win, so they did not go the polls to cast a ballot. Pete's friends did not consider this young opponent a real threat to the office and position that Pete held. They may have been surprised but not as much as Daddy.

He was not just disappointed, he was personally hurt. He did not expect the apathy to be so wide spread. Even as a beginning lawyer in town, he always encouraged people to speak up, to exercise their voting rights as citizens. Had the encouragement fallen on deaf ears? This was a prime example of Daddy always championing a cause for rights and freedom. When asked if he would ask for a recount, his reply was just, "The people have spoken."

Honoring Mayor Simmons

During the May 1, 1967 Council meeting this was recorded in the minutes:

Mayor Simmons spoke a few words concerning the ups-and-downs during his term as Mayor of the City of Broken Arrow. He thanked the Council members who had served with him for their assistance. Mayor Simmons stated he did not feel one is ever was able to accomplish all one intended during a term of office and he was no exception.

Vice-Mayor Gesin read a resolution in recognition of the "unselfish dedication and "Qualities of Leadership" evidenced by Mayor Paul (Pete) Simmons during his term of office, and, for this untiring effort in behalf of the welfare of the citizens of Broken Arrow. Motion by Dr. Newcomb, seconded by Mr. Helms for adoption of this resolution. All for, motion carried. Mayor Simmons was then presented a plaque with gavel in appreciation of his services to the City.

Dr. James Newcomb, a Loyal Friend

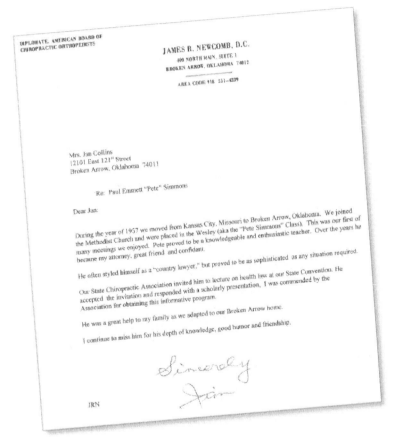

Dr. Newcomb was a loyal long time friend.

A New Start

No matter what reasons were given for the loss in this mayoral race, the bottom line was Pete felt his hometown disappointed and partly embarrassed him by not showing up on election day to vote. It was loud and clear to him they did not care. He felt as if his hometown had betrayed him. Pete began planning the direction in which he should go. He already had two children leave home for college and then one of those two for the military. He may have even had thoughts of people asking over and over about the election, expressing their remorse and not wanting to continue to hear the excuses they called legitimate reasons.

Pete Pays for Mama's College

In 1969 he decided to make a new start, a clean break. After all, he had left Broken Arrow once before under difference circumstances that were beyond his control. This time, he made his own decision. Fran had always wanted to continue her education, but had been unable to do so since he was busy building his law practice and she had to assist him in between secretaries. Barbara was graduating soon and starting college in the fall. Daddy thought it would be logical to just move to a college town instead of having Fran to commute. They made plans to move to Tahlequah, Oklahoma.

After practicing law for 20 years in Broken Arrow,
Paul E. 'Pete' Simmons turned the page in Tahlequah.

Chapter 18
A NEW CHAPTER IN SERVANTHOOD

Chris and I attended Northeastern State College before it became a university. Barbara would most likely attend there also. I helped Mother enroll for the fall semester. Fran entered college as a 50 year old freshman. Several Broken Arrow students were her classmates. Richard Spradling often mentions what fun they had in the classes they attended.

The Markham house was an 1905 southern-style home.
• Used by permission Talequah Press/Pictorial Press

So plans were finalized and the move was made in 1969. The house Pete and Fran were able to acquire in Tahlequah was the Markham home. A 1905 stately structure, it was on northeastern Oklahoma's register for historic homes. The home was rumored to have been the scene of a murder, which made great conversation to add to Pete's repertoire of unique stories.

Open For Business

After practicing law for almost twenty years in Broken Arrow, Pete left what he considered his hometown, hung out his shingle once again as a new beginning in 1970. His office was located on Water Street. It did not take him long to have clients. An article appeared in the Tahlequah Pictorial Press announcing the opening of his office.

Pete's Reputation Precedes Him

He was not that far from his hometown and many other Broken Arrow graduates enrolled there. Ronnie and Linda (Johnson) Penny were among the married students at NSC during that time and recalled an incident in which they were involved. There was an article in the paper in which a 'Linda Pinney' had been arrested and was in the Tahlequah jail. Although that was not the same Linda who was from Broken Arrow, word traveled quickly back home to her parents. As people will, someone asked Linda's mother, Virginia Johnson of the Arkansas Valley State Bank what had happened to Linda. Virginia called the young couple to make sure Linda

Pete hung out his shingle and started afresh in Tahlequah, Oklahoma.
• Used by permission
Tahlequah Pictorial Press

was all right. Afterwards Linda assured her mother the person who was jailed was not the same Linda. After a couple of people inquired, Virginia called her daughter back and told Linda to "Call Pete Simmons. He's practicing law there in Tahlequah now." It did not take long before the newspaper retracted their statement with an apology. Pete always got things done. He never lacked for business.

A New Chapter of Servanthood

It was not long before Pete saw a need. Several Native American people began coming to him for his services. However, he realized that many of these Cherokee people spoke little or no English. He immediately began resolving that situation. He went to the college campus and got a schedule for classes to be offered the very next semester. He enrolled in a Cherokee Language Class and learned how to speak Cherokee.

The Cherokee people were impressed Pete would actually care enough to take the time to enroll in a class to learn their language. He won their hearts in reaching out to the native people of the Cherokee Nation and they in turn brought their friends and family to his office for legal work.

At the time, Cherokee County was not as affluent as Tulsa County so there was also a need for court-appointed attorneys, for those who cannot afford to hire an attorney of their own. He had plenty of Pro Bono ("for the good of the people") business in Tahlequah.

Pete always had a desire to give and help others because of that gift of service placed in him by God. I believe it also helped to fulfill the desire of being needed in his personal life. He may have felt if Broken Arrow doesn't need me anymore, I will find a place that does need me. And he did.

Leaving the Door Open

Pete kept the building at 323 South Main, maintained a home in Broken Arrow and eventually did business with hometown folks again when he was back in town. But he did most of his law practice in Tahlequah until the family graduated from college.

My folks would come back to Broken Arrow on the weekends to attend church and Daddy taught Sunday School. This time he taught a high school class. Being back in town seemed to be a workable situation and Daddy could stay connected with Broken Arrow.

Practicing law in Tahlequah was a good experience for him. Daddy's inclination was to be a servant to his community and helped the Cherokee people and others with legal services. He was very effective and appreciated by his clients.

Local Speed Trap

Anyone who has attended Northeastern State University for the last fifty years or more knows Hulbert, a small town in Cherokee County, was most known for their speed trap going through town. Speed traps lead to issuing tickets and court dates. Court dates resulted in seeking out services for a capable attorney. Pete had plenty of business for speeding tickets.

The 1960s and 1970s were days before sophisticated technology like speed detection radar was affordable, especially for small towns. When appearing before the judge in city court in Hulbert people had a difficult time getting their speeding tickets dismissed or even reduced in the charge. Without absolute proof, it could be one's word against another's, namely the driver versus the police officer. There is a difference between trying to adjust one's speed accordingly, driving about five miles over the limit or blatantly not observing the speed limit at all.

As proficient as he was in his profession, Pete had difficulty at times getting tickets dismissed or feeling as if he were assisting his clients as best as he could. Although he may have felt as he was right, but could not prove it. He was always searching for solutions to problems, his and others. His solution to the problem in Hulbert was to assist them in acquiring a radar gun for the city. It may have reduced the city's revenue somewhat, but he felt as if it brought fairness to each situation based on is own merits after that. It was now based on more accurate evidence. Pete may have had happier clients and won more cases after that point.

Welcome Home, Sailor!

Kenny Collins and I met and began dating in 1971. He drove to Tahlequah from Broken Arrow to spend Christmas Eve with my family when he was home on leave from the United States Navy. This occasion was the first time he had really met my parents. Like a good dad inspecting this prospect to determine if he was worthy of dating his daughter, Pete met Kenny at the front door. But this particular father met Kenny at the front door holding a hand gun. His welcoming sentence was, "Look what I got Jan's mother for Christmas." Never allowing anyone to intimidate him, Kenny just nodded, "Nice," and walked on past him. Pete always liked for people to be bold enough to stand up to him. During the course of the evening Daddy asked Kenny if he knew the Marine Corps' 200th birthday celebration was coming in just four years? Without missing a beat, Kenny's reply was, "Yes sir, Marines have been guarding Navy gates for almost 200 years and they've only lost one." Kenny showed Pete from the very beginning he had his own style of humor.

That was the beginning of a long time relationship. They understood each other from the very beginning of their relationship. Through the years, Kenny learned how to fix things and Daddy was always in need of having things repaired. There was not much Daddy attempted and could not achieve. He was not mechanically inclined, nor did he care to be.

Kenny recalls his bachelor party at which only four men attended and were entertained by Pete's stories. Daddy warned him, "she is just like me."

Enjoying the banter, with quick wit Kenny quipped, "I can say something you will never be able to say."

Of course Pete asked, "What's that?" Kenny's reply was, "I can say my daughter never married a sailor!" Laughter was always something Daddy enjoyed.

Pete and Kenny pulled a surprise prank at our wedding with the 'proverbial shotgun' which at one time belonged to his Grandma Neighbors.

Celebrating in his law office with co-workers after winning the Wagoner County Associate District Judge election.
• Courtesy of Broken Arrow Ledger

Chapter 19
HERE COME DA JUDGE

The first time Daddy ran for Associate District Judge in Wagoner County in 1976, he was defeated by a small margin. He ran again in 1978 against the same incumbent judge. Pete Simmons cleverly incorporated information from an editorial written by an unidentified source in the Broken Arrow Ledger into an ad that he placed in the Wagoner County Record Democrat on August 21, 1978. He succinctly explained the reasons why he was running by simply underlining, highlighting and circling specific paragraphs from the editorial, which were reasons he recognized as good. Pete felt very strongly about all people, but specifically here the people of Wagoner County not being properly represented.

It's Time to Change Judges
'Judge Not, Judge!'

In the midst of a campaign season muddled by more slime than usual, we find a charge in an ad published in some Wagoner County newspapers a little more than unusual.

It concerns candidates for a district judgeship.

This ad contains a long list of cases, by numbers, naming the offenses alleged committed by clients of one candidate for the post. In the vast majority of most of the cases listed, all charges apparently were dismissed.

It doesn't spell it out, but it implies guilt by association...that a defense attorney somehow is painted with the same reputation as the client he is defending... who may or may not be guilty.

Nothing could be more opposite from our American system of justice, which holds that every man is innocent until he is proven guilty, that every man is entitled to a fair and just trial before a jury of his peers, and that he is entitled to an attorney who can help guarantee that he will get a fair and just trial. A defense attorney does that, nothing more.

Those of us who are for law and order and the orderly punishment of the wrongdoers in our society are strong in our defense of our American justice system and for the rights of those accused, whoever he may be, to have legal counsel. That is basic in the Bill of Rights.

Further to imply that there is something shady in dismissal of a case even more a base attempt to mislead the voters. The defense attorney does not dismiss the case... the prosecuting attorney does when he cannot make a case, the judge does when he does not see enough evidence.

Wagoner County voters are a sophisticated lot. We do not think they will fall for the implications in this type of advertising.

We think they will agree with us. It is even more reprehensible that it should be placed by a judge himself, an attorney ... and who should know the place of an attorney in the courtroom.

[Note: Pete wrote the words "We agree!" in the margin of the circled paragraphs.]

It's Time to for a Change!
Elect Paul E. (Pete) Simmons
Associate District Judge
(paid for by Paul E. (Pete) Simmons)

Simmons Hopes to Speed Justice

The Broken Arrow Ledger said this about Pete's reasons for running for election in this article:

We just have to streamline the way we handle these cases in our courts," says Paul (Pete) Simmons…
The docket for traffic and misdemeanor cases in Wagoner County stretches over 70 pages… It is inconceivable to me that Wagoner County should have a docket substantially larger than the City of Tulsa….
Citizens of Wagoner County are not getting a fair shake…It's a waste of peoples' money when cases are delayed or continued with due justification.
…Simmons says his only reason for getting into the race is to guarantee justice… when I see something that needs to be done," he claims.

In the second bid for Associate District Judge, it was three-man race. Paul E. "Pete" Simmons won in a run-off election and took office in January, 1979.

Simmons Memoirs

I cannot adequately tell about Daddy's experiences on the bench as Wagoner Country Associate District Judge without mentioning his bailiff, Deborah Linzy Overstreet, who came to my dad for a job right out of high school. She wrote this about the experience she had on her first day in his courtroom:

As a recent high school graduate and newly married, I was searching for employment when an employee with a job training program referred me to the Wagoner County Courthouse. On a summer morning in May, I was told to wait on the bench on the second floor of the Wagoner County Courthouse for "the judge." At 8:00 a.m., a spry gentleman with a slight limp came down the stairs from the third floor. He smiled at me and asked, "Young lady, may I help you?" I told him the job training program had sent me for a job interview. He asked if I could type and when I answered in the affirmative, at 17 years of age, I was hired as courtroom bailiff by Associate District Judge Paul E. (Pete) Simmons. That was truly the most important decision of my career. Judge Simmons was more than my boss. He was my professor, my mentor and my surrogate father.

I can truly say my first day as Judge Simmons' bailiff is forever etched in my mind. Included on the docket for the day was a non-jury trial fish and game case. The state alleged that a gentleman had been fishing by illegally electrocuting fish, or in non-layman's terms, "telephoning". The officer had seized the equipment that was used by the gentleman by "telephoning" for the fish, which included the battery system and telescoping net. During the trial the Assistant District Attorney proceeded to extend the pole on the net to prove the length the gentleman went to reach the stunned fish. There was testimony from the gentleman and trial became quite intense. At the end of the trial, Judge Simmons found the gentleman guilty and assessed a fine and court costs. The gentleman asked for return of his property. Judge Simmons agreed to return of the telescoping net, but refused return of the illegal electrocution system, to which the Assistant District Attorney vehemently objected, claiming that both items had been taken during the act of a crime and should remain as property of the state. Disgruntled, the Assistant District Attorney begins packing away his trial documents in his briefcase, muttering under his breath. Meanwhile, the gentleman begins collapsing the pole on the net with his back to the Assistant District Attorney. You can just imagine my surprise when the gentleman unknowingly hits the Assistant District Attorney in the back of the head with the pole! The Assistant District Attorney swings around and lunges for the gentleman, claiming that the gentleman hit him on purpose. Judge Simmons is yelling for me to call the Sheriff. I am glued to my chair, eyes wide open! I jumped to my feet and run for the telephone in the Judge's chambers. But there is one major problem: I don't know the Sheriff's telephone number! To this day the Wagoner County Sheriff's telephone number is one I have never forgotten!

Debbie was with Judge Simmons in the courtroom every day and saw his actions and every move he made until the end of his term. I knew her perspective was important in describing how he ran his courtroom and conducted himself around the courthouse. One of the first times we met to discuss this chapter, she told me every morning when Judge Simmons arrived at the Wagoner County Courthouse, he first went to check on the juveniles to make sure they had been fed and given an adequate amount of food.

Another Personal Witness

Many eyewitnesses could easily step up and testify to the character and expertise Daddy exhibited on the bench as the Associate District Judge of Wagoner County during his term of office. However, because some of Daddy's colleagues and contemporaries are no longer living, I asked Debbie Overstreet who would have known him well enough in the Wagoner area to assist me in collecting accurate information. She suggested I contact Judge Dennis Shook, the current Wagoner County Associate District Judge. When I called Judge Shook's office, I learned he had taken some time off to visit his mother in another state. Much to my surprise, he called me while on vacation which I deeply appreciated.

Judge Dennis N. Shook shared his knowledge of and experiences with my dad:

I first appeared before Judge Simmons as a young lawyer, right out of law school after passing the bar exam only three to four months prior to that. The Judge had been elected in 1978 and took office in 1979.

About a year later I appeared before him on another case in 1980. He not only impressed me with his knowledge of the law but with his incredible memory. He not only remembered me, but the specific case I was on as well.

He was very personable and we readily became friends. As a native Iowan, I had come to the University of Tulsa to attend law school.

I discovered that he occasionally called people by nicknames. I became known as "Hawkeye" to him. I was Associate District Attorney for Wagoner County when I mostly came in contact with him in court.

Pete had an incredibly broad knowledge of law—there was no area that he did not have expertise in— criminal, family, probates, oil and gas lease. He had a great deal of competence and knew more law than any other judges I had ever known.

He was a wonderful judge and an excellent mentor. I learned so much from him. I had a lot of respect for him as an individual and as a judge. He was very ambitious but compassionate. He was always willing to hear cases presented before him.

He brought to the bench years and years of experience. He could have been a judge long before he did, but he came in the twilight of his career.

He had a remarkable record as Wagoner County Associate District Judge. One major thing that was extremely impressive. He was never reversed on an appeal. That not only speaks in high regard for his record but about his decisions as well.

Everyone knew Pete was a very controversial public figure. Judge Shook and I had to sadly agree Daddy created a lot of his own attention that was given to the controversy. He enjoyed being an individualist and above all a nonconformist. Judge Simmons never backed down from his opinions when they stood for justice but may have unknowingly opened a door to negativity stemming from his unique but unusual humor and personality which resulted in negative attention in the press.

Courtroom Antics

Not everyone is aware of the many negative articles that were written by various newspapers in Oklahoma about Judge

Simmons. The main things people remember are the stories written about his quirkiness in eating cheese and crackers or spreading raw hamburger meat on the crackers with his Marine knife during court sessions. Daddy always ate his beef rare and occasionally ate it raw at home. It was not unusual to family members. Although that may have appeared to be an attention-getting antic, his opponents overlooked the fact he worked through his lunch hour to serve the people of Wagoner County in completing his docket each day. He was adhering to the law as closely as he could by allowing the people "the right of a quick and speedy trial."

Found Guilty

There were times juveniles became disruptive in the courtroom and Judge Simmons felt he had to give them a strong object lesson by telling them of his experience in the Louisiana State Penitentiary or by saying, "You think you're tough. I'll show you 'tough." proceeding to exhibit one of his famous cigarette tricks performed as a former Boy Scout Master as remembered and described earlier by former scout David Hartman.

It was not unusual for Judge Simmons to 'match the sentence to fit the crime.' He sentenced many juveniles to do community service instead of putting them behind bars, depending on severity of their offense. There were times he sentenced their parents to do community service as well and work alongside their children. He believed surely both would take this sentence seriously and understand the mercy which was extended to give them a second chance.

Patricia Hanlon, Tulsa World correspondent interviewed

Judge Simmons, after his retirement and wrote this:

Simmons continues to be a staunch defender of the poor. 'The poor are often given a raw deal,' said Simmons. A teenage girl was once picked up for truancy and sent to Judge Simmons' court in Wagoner... [after telling her his stories of being a railroad bum] he lectured her on the folly of running away. 'After that, she quit her vagrant ways,' he said.

Simmons sentenced misdemeanor offenders to community service long before it was law to do so. He had offenders busy polishing court room floors, washing police cars and digging dandelions on public property.

Once, a woman was charged for disturbing the peace. Simmons told her what she did was childish. In lieu of a fine, she had to write 500 times on the blackboard, "I will not disturb the peace."

"There she was writing and crying while I went down to check on her every few minutes," said Simmons.

Years ago, Simmons said he sentenced a young man guilty of an impulsive act of violence.

In declaring the sentence, Simmons told him, 'I hope, in your case, you'll come back from prison a better man.'

The young man thanked him and shook Simmons' hand.

"He was touched because someone cared," said Simmons.

"To this day, that still brings tears to my eyes," said Simmons.

CYCLE RIDING JUDGE - Associate District Judge Paul Simmons is doing his part to conserve energy by driving his Suzuki 400 motorcycle to work every day. Simmons drives a 50-mile trip every day to the Wagoner County Courthouse. "Every day I drive over the Ben Lumpkin road," Simmons said. Simmons pointed out that he isn't the only one conserving energy. He said deputy Dallas Thompson and dispatcher Ralph Rose also drive their motorcycles to work. The 64-year-old judge said Dennis Greg Johnson also commutes to work on a motorcycle. Simmons said it costs him about $1 a day to ride his motorcycle.

Pete began riding a motorcycle to court at age 64.

Cycling Riding Judge

A picture and article appeared in The Wagoner Tribune about Pete riding his motorcycle to court:

240

Cycling Riding Judge—Associate District Judge Paul Simmons is doing his part to conserve energy by driving his Suzuki 350 motorcycle to work every day. Simmons drives a 50-mile trip every day to the Wagoner Country Courthouse.

'Every day I drive over the Ben Lumpkin Road,' Simmons said. Simmons pointed out he is not the only one conserving energy. He said deputy Dallas Thompson and dispatcher Ralph Rose also ride their motorcycles to work. The 64-year-old judge said Dentist Greg Johnson also commutes to work on a motorcycle. Simmons said it costs him about $1.00 a day to ride his motorcycle.

Later he sold his Suzuki 350 and drove a motorcycle with an automatic transmission before he retired. It was a CB750A Hondamatic. There was an article in the Globe Magazine about his cycling to work.

Happy Birthday, Judge

Pete celebrated his 70th birthday in 1984 during his second term as Associated District Judge in Wagoner County.

Debbie Overstreet probably initiated the party, but she and Suzanne Lau joined forces to write up a special poem for him:

The Living Legend

Ladies and Gentlemen, one and all,
The story of our boss is one that sounds tall.
While life as a Judge may sound complete,
It's the rest of his story we must repeat.

Starting his life as a rodeo clown
Must have pleasured many a town.
While dangerous a job, It's been rumored,
To him added character, his sense of humor.

From there he advanced to a railroad bum,
This story he repeats with a smile and a hum,
Hopping freight trains, his destiny did take,
A course that would make the rest of us quake.
Traveling across the U.S. of A.,
A myriad of experiences, who's to say?

But finally Prodigal Pete did alight,
And would not you know it, in the middle of a fight!
The Marines take only the best, as you know
So, of course, our boss was the first to go.
On the Island of Guadalcanal risked his life,
Still alive due to his trusty trench knife.

In 1950 the Bar he did take,
A career in Law, thirty-three years to date,
Still adhering to 'never retreat'
Earned him the nickname of 'Ole Pistol Pete'!

What kind of man did this life make?
It's tough to explain, but we'll give it a shake,
Makes for a man with a trench knife does eat,
Salted crackers and raw hamburger meat,

Yet, no wiser, or warmer, or kinder a man
Has ever walked the face of this land,
He's quite a "character", I've heard some say,

AN OKLAHOMA ORIGINAL

· ·

Correction! A "Living Legend" in every way!

We love you!

Suzanne Lau
Debra Helsey (Overstreet)

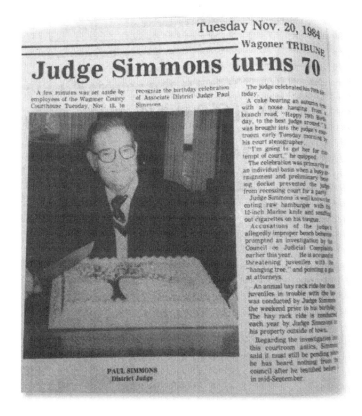

Judge Simmons celebrating his 70th birthday
• Use by permission Wagoner Tribune

The Wagoner Tribune quoted Judge Simmons: In referring to Suzanne and Debbie, he said "I should find them in contempt of court for this act," looking at them and smiling.

Restoration of Family

Judge Simmons had many cases involving divorce and family matters. He did his best to be fair and impartial. I met a young man recently who told me about his particular case with Daddy. Leland Grubb related a touching story about how his divorce was granted by Judge Simmons after much deliberation about intent. Daddy did his very best to counsel and encourage a couple to reconcile their differences, especially for the sake of the children. Sometimes it was difficult to achieve that. Leland was granted his divorce and later returned to the courtroom for custody of his children. He told me Judge Simmons let him know 'if at all possible, those children need to remain with their mother.' Because of an absentee mother, who refused to appear in court on several different occasions, he ruled in favor of Leland. With emotion, Leland shared with me that it was not easy, but he learned how to rear his children from a homemaker's perspective as well as the father's.

Another story told by Lynn Bertling and Carol Hocutt Bertling, two friends of mine. Still feeling how special Daddy was to them, they shared how Judge Simmons granted both of their divorces on separate occasions. On the verge of tears and shaking, Carol said the judge asked her, "Are you certain this is what you want to do?" Of course, she did not want to, but felt it was necessary, replied in the affirmative. They laughed as they told me there was a happy ending to this story because Daddy later joined Lynn and Carol in their new marriage and life together.

A Rewarding Experience

Serving as Associate District Judge of Wagoner County for the State of Oklahoma was a rewarding experience for Judge

Simmons for the better part of five years.

When *The Tulsa World* reported his death, they contacted me. I told them I believed the negative press literally broke his heart. It is a sad day when a person tries his best to help humanity and is ridiculed in the midst of it.

Simmons announce re-election plans

associate district judge post. The 57-year-old judge said he would never retire even if he were not on the bench. He said he would continue his former job as a trial lawyer and referred to an adage written on a rock in his chambers, "Old lawyers don't die they just lose their appeal."

"I'm not sure I can survive another four years, but I'm gonna try awful hard," Simmons said. "My health isn't bad but it's not good either."

Simmons said he suffered under stress after taking office but now says he has the problems ironed out. After hiring a bailiff and court reporter some of the problems were solved.

The courtroom is referred to as "The Pit" by lawyers, Simmons said, because the analogy is similar to that of fighters in a ring. He said his job is that of a referee while the lawyers are adversaries for their clients.

Simmons said he doesn't have any high accomplishments he can point to during his ...

a speedy trial and certainly of punishment if a defendent was guilty.

The position of associate district judge covers all jurisdictions but the one Simmons said gives him the most enjoyment is juvenile. He said he feels more like a social worker and is able to see results of his job and hopes he influences lives for the better.

Divorce cases are the heaviest docket Simmons has but mental health cases are the ones he likes least. The reason he detests mental cases is because of the nature of the case and because it is hard to determine a means for improvement.

Other areas of juris Simmons has ... adoptions, ... probates, small civil cases, ... hearings ... or crim... felonie... Adult ...

"Everyone is ... courtesy and ... important ... associate dis... tion are the ... courage ... patience ... Simmons ...

Simmons ... part of his ... with ev... said th... charac... make...

JUDGE PAUL E. SIMMONS

Incumbent Associate District Judge Paul E. Simmons has announced his candidacy for re-election.

Pete continued to be dedicated to streamline the court docket, promoting 'Citizens' right to a fair and speedy trial.'
• Used by permission Wagoner Tribune

Chapter 20
PRIDE COMES BEFORE A FALL

Choleric personalities such as Pete's not only project an image of boldness but appear to be prideful as well. Without trying to over analyze, through the years I have noticed in Daddy and others with his personality often times they show that outward appearance in actuality to overcompensate for a sensitive nature. As others may agree, Pete never willingly showed weakness.

That may sound unusual, but because Pete was forced out of the nest at such a young age, it could have caused some of those attributes. He became a survivor in so many ways and a real overachiever in others. He was truly gifted as a lawyer and judge so there was no lack of confidence there. He simply guarded his heart and did not allow that many people inside his world of emotions and true feelings. I have learned through observing Daddy over the years.

Family Evangelism Brought Full Circle

Although the focus of this book is about Pete Simmons' life and career, it also is about going beyond the image and sharing the heart of this unique man. I would be remiss if I only told part of the story that brought me to the point of sharing his complete story.

While growing up, I must have missed some religious training. I first remember Reverend A.D. Gregory in the early 1950's preaching strong and powerful sermons at First Methodist Church in Broken Arrow. I do not recall what the messages were exactly, because I was very young at the time. However, my mother told me several years later, I would line up my dolls and preach to them.

Mrs. Lillian Mahaffey was special to me. As my third grade Sunday School teacher, she taught us the books of the Bible. She gave us a little white New Testament at the end of the year after we made our recitation of all sixty-six books in front of the whole church body. I also loved Mrs. Lucy Bright, my sweet Sunday School teacher from the fourth grade. I did not know until years later, she was the sister-in-law of Bill Bright, the founder of Campus Crusade for Christ.

But something happened in my understanding between those years and the years of later ministers. I lost some of the teaching and training and somehow did not catch the whole meaning of confirmation. I did not have a solid foundation, but when my father-in-law, Paul C. Collins gave me a small pamphlet about salvation, I understood salvation better.

Not knowing the whole story about the revival Daddy's family attended in 1923, his parents' divorce and the subsequent breakdown of his family, I was very naive about not being too exuberant about my new experience.

My new journey ironically continued in the same First Methodist Church where I was nurtured as a child. It was developed by attending a ladies' Bible study class with Beverly Turnipseed teaching as well as Reverend Charles Puckett's preaching as pastor. It was no doubt the greatest revelation I have ever had but not everyone shared in my excitement.

During Sunday dinner at my parents' house, shortly after my conversion, I innocently but ignorantly made a comment or spoke a religious phrase in front of everyone present. I was not prepared for what transpired that day. Had I known more about my dad's upbringing, his being shifted from home to home during his high school years and his California, Missouri experience, maybe I would have been more sensitive to the issue. But I knew none of that at the time.

Daddy's comment to me was I was talking and acting too religious as his mother had. I did not realize that day brought many years of pain and emotion to the surface for him. He did not know I felt some personal rejection from him that day too until we talked years later. Because it was an upsetting event, I felt like the best thing to do that day was to leave. I gathered my six-month-old baby, her diaper bag and belongings, and left their house with my husband, Kenny. That event hurt both of us in different ways. It is an example of how we perceive a situation which can affect what we believe.

"Wilt Thou Be Healed?"

From 1976, the spring my dad shocked me with those devastating words, until Father's Day, June 16, 1984, there were no significant religious or spiritual conversations between Daddy and me.

The week prior to Father's Day, 1984, Daddy had been in the Broken Arrow Hospital on Elm Place. He waited until we were all present and shared with the entire immediate family he had prostate cancer.

The morning of Father's Day, I was thinking of how our visit to Broken Arrow would transpire because of the recent medical report Daddy received. But as I was putting my contacts in my eyes, I dropped one down the drain. Not wanting to be late to church I put the other contact in my eye and headed out the door. During service, the pastor called people to the altar with prayer needs. A thought came to me to ask for prayer to find my contact, but I rejected the thought as a silly request.

Unexpectedly, I felt impressed to remove the single contact from my eye. As I did, I looked up and my eyesight was perfectly normal. Feeling grateful for a sudden miracle of healing, I realized part of the purpose was for me to understand if it happened to me, it could also happen to Daddy. I felt as if it was a mandate I must do.

I had a sudden wave of fear at the mere thought of approaching my daddy with this suggestion. Composure and peace returned to me as I felt God was bringing me to a place in my life to minister back and bring restoration to one of His sheep, my daddy Paul Emmett Simmons.

The evening before daddy had surgery, I went to visit him at St. Francis Hospital in Tulsa. I shared with him what had happened to my eyes on Father's Day. Surprisingly, Daddy received my words. With a tear in his eye, he replied, "There has been no doubt in my mind He could and would." And God did. Daddy had a successful surgery with no complications and after a follow-up examination, the doctors reported that Pete was cancer-free.

I Whipped Cancer

A year later, I overheard my dad talking to a cousin at a family funeral in Tulsa. As if he were counting the notches on his gun-slinging belt, he boasted confidently, "I whipped cancer and the D.A.'s office all in one year." I literally cringed when I heard those words. I wanted to shake him and say, "Pete, did you not learn anything from the ordeal you went through with cancer?"

But I could not say anything. I only knew one must give credit to whom credit is due and one should give glory to whom glory is due. It saddened me that day to hear those words. I hoped and prayed this was not the beginning of opening the door to more physical challenges in Daddy's life.

After he received bad press, Judge Simmons retired from the bench;
he went back into private practice.

• Used by permission Tulsa World correspondent, Patricia Hanlon
(from p. 238 when I quoted Pete from her interview)

Pete showing the grandchildren what a real cowboy looked like,
...hat, jeans and bathrobe?

Chapter 21
BACK IN THE SADDLE AGAIN

The Fight of His Life

Often people recognize someone's personality early in his or her life. It was true in Judge Simmons' case. Even as a student at Tulsa Central High School, whoever wrote the caption for his senior picture pegged him right. The phrase 'A likable chap who possesses pluck and ambition and a fighting spirit' certainly fit him to a T. The Broken Arrow Ledger's reporter, Joan Rose, wrote this about Pete in a final article:

Although he was never taken by surprise, he knew he was in for a fight. He recalls that during his first election "it wasn't the first time he received 'bad press,' but this time Pete felt it was particularly unfair. "They could not keep me from being what I've always been. I have never avoided anything," he said many times.

Even after he won the election, the bad press did not stop. He often felt that the Tulsa papers were ridiculing him as a 'country lawyer,' they called him gun-toting, knife-toting, grandstanding."

It still did not keep him from 'being himself,' and he was always proud of his judicial record. He counseled the young people who came before him and he made believers out of them.

He showed the juveniles what being 'tough' was like, and convinced them that they only thought they wanted to be…

The Good the Bad and the Ugly

Judge Simmons felt as if he was making the right decisions and pronouncing the proper judgments. Instead he received unjust assaults on his character through statements made by his opponents. When one is in the public eye, there will always be criticism. When one joins the political arena, there will always be those who do not agree with others. According to the Second Amendment of our Constitution, we are always afforded our freedom of speech. There have been many people in our society who have had their careers ruined by assumption of guilt and poor character by the media. As often as it happens, not everyone realizes stories printed in newspapers or reported over the airwaves may not be entirely true. News generally has a slant; reporters do not always check out their sources or report both sides of an issue.

Daddy referred to The Tulsa Tribune in his video interview as "ironically the place he had his first job." When articles were written about him in the Tulsa newspapers, he was disappointed that reporters did not check out the facts or had ever sat in his courtroom. However, he did feel supported when people attempted to correct bad press by writing editorials like this one:

This editorial appeared in the Tulsa Tribune:

Judge's Positive Side

Editor, The Tribune: I read with interest recently a third article concerning Judge Paul Simmons of the Wagoner County District Court…Your writers seem to take great pleasure in making a mockery of some of the innocuous antics of a very fine jurist. They have also engaged in some heavy criticism of the man's treatment of certain cases. I do not take issue with the right of the press to criticize, but I feel constrained to offer some positive input in defense of Judge Simmons; ...

Judge Simmons has always been extremely cordial and accommodating to me in terms of conducting hearings and working around my schedule... On other occasions Judge Simmons has shown an interest in the welfare of the citizenry that far surpasses what most of us would expect from a man in his position... The concern he shows is more than superficial.

In defense of the judge's antics, I would offer that he has been a member of the legal profession for many years and has a proven track record... I believe the judge has been attacked by some attorneys who cannot understand his attitude toward the administration of justice. Rather than adhering always to the "letter" of the law. "Pete" Simmons metes out justice more often than not in accordance with the "spirit of it."

When we are facing a judge like "Pete" Simmons I think some of us must fear the simple fact that he is less swayed by our persuasive arguments than by the evidence itself...

Judge Simmons has proved time and again that his greatest concern is for the well-being of the people of that county. If that is a fault, may more of us be cursed with the same infirmity.

R.C.O., Tulsa

Time to Hang up His Gloves

After allegations were brought by his opponents for personal reasons, which Judge Simmons called 'half-truths' and not legitimate issues, they began proceedings to remove him from the bench. Daddy's attorneys encouraged him to take a medical retirement. The physical, mental but mostly the emotional wear of the accusations took a toll on his health again. So, against what his 'fighting spirit' dictated to him he accepted the advice of his attorneys. Debbie Overstreet told me that it was ironic but unfortunate the three main attorneys who brought charges against Pete were eventually disbarred from practicing law.

Back in the Saddle Again

Daddy retired from the bench in 1985 but went back into private practice defending the common man once again no matter whether poor, hopeless or able. He had an office in Coweta for the next few years and brought his bailiff, Debra Overstreet, along with him as his legal secretary.

Debbie has expressed a great deal of gratitude to Daddy as a professional example, a mentor. As she observed Judge Simmons ruling from the bench with his knowledge of the law she felt surpassed others, she absorbed all she could learn. Later, she became a paralegal and now works for the Corps of Engineers in Tulsa, Oklahoma.

New Associates

One of Daddy's new associates was Robert Waller, a retired Air Force officer. After military retirement, he attended law school at the University of Tulsa. He was truly a gentleman, and another lawyer who enjoyed Pete's mentoring. After Daddy retired, Waller continued practicing law there in the office just south of the Green Parrot Café on Broadway in Coweta, Oklahoma.

Mazzio Days

There were times when I was not working or teaching school, and was able to go to Coweta to have lunch with him. Those were special times, between 1988 and 1992 when I felt like we reconnected. Daddy did not have the busy workload he had in previous years. He was not as driven to make a living or in a hurry to rush to court. I discovered he actually had the time to slow down enough for more than a 30-minute lunch break. Those were the days we really enjoyed reminiscing and learned to know and appreciate one another. Most of the time we went to Mazzio's to eat salad and pizza.

As we visited, I realized he had never really shared with me details of his experience in the United States Marine Corps. I knew the names of most of the islands where he was stationed, but was never familiar with duties he performed. I had seen island pictures but never considered war zones where he may have been. As he shared with me his main assignment, he expressed regret of not doing his fair share of combat. When he told me about his experience being chosen for the enormous task of organizing the mail to servicemen on many different islands, I had an opportunity to tell him what an honor and important job delivering mail really was. He was not only able to serve his beloved country in one area, but helped build the moral of soldiers over several islands. Mail from home boosted their self-esteem like nothing else could and kept their hopes alive.

While sharing our lunchtimes together Daddy told me more about his life growing up than he ever had shared before. I learned more about him: 'the man behind the image', the complex one. He began telling me about the events and people who affected, molded and influenced his life. I always felt as if I knew and understood Daddy more than others did, but I still felt there was something missing. It was the puzzle with the missing pieces. Those were the days I was able to put most of the puzzle pieces together and figure out this complicated individual who I had called my dad for over forty-five years.

A Covenant Remembered

It was during those times I learned for the first time he rode with Grandpa Neighbors in the 1924 Tourister around the towns to hear him preach the gospel to rural areas that had no preacher. He told me he had wanted to be a preacher. When I inquired, he said he did not follow that direction because he said he cried very easily. He was afraid he would be asked to preach a funeral and would not be able to fulfill that duty because he might break down and cry.

Those lunches became very precious events to me because he shared it was during his early years he was saved and filled with the spirit. That was something I had never known. I did not question anything he said. I was just surprised because it seemed as if he had rejected any philosophy or religion to which his mother adhered.

Over salad and pizza we discussed opinions and philosophies and the hypothetical "what ifs." I told him I thought he would have done a wonderful job as a preacher. I also boldly told him it was what I believed to be God's will and direction for him. We were able to speak honestly with each other. I was just as opinionated as he was.

It was also in Coweta and our Mazzio days when we discussed how God allows us to follow our own paths….. I believe He never imposes His will on us, but He does have a perfect plan for our lives if we choose to follow it.

Most people would say they felt like Pete followed the profession he was supposed to because he was so good at what he did. At the time I believed if he helped that many people in a court of law, how many more people could he have persuaded and influenced from a pulpit.

Truth vs. Perception

As I recall, the first conversation my dad and I had about truth versus perception was when we pondered the strongest word we know. I told him "truth" is the most important word we would ever know. He, however, disagreed. He said perception is a stronger word because what people perceive the truth to be has greater influence over them than the actual truth. I did not agree with him then, but looking back at that day, I understand now what he meant. Even from the time I began writing this book until now, I have altered my perception about Daddy. It is amazing how research and looking at the total picture of one's life can influence and continue to affect my own perception.

Debbie Overstreet comments nearly every time I see her how much Daddy enjoyed our time together at Mazzio's in Coweta. She said he loved our discussions and bantering back and forth. Obviously I took it more seriously than he did. I was just glad to see him back in the saddle again doing what he loved. As good a judge as I think he was, I believe he enjoyed defending people as well.

Pete enjoyed relaxing after work on his farm with grandkids.

Chapter 22
DOWN ON THE FARM

When Mother and Daddy moved to the farm, it was one of the greatest joys Daddy had. He liked being outdoors and was a modern-day cowboy. The grandchildren were young or continuing to be born and those were memorable times.

Kim, Chris' daughter, was their first grandchild. That always holds a special place in the hearts of grandparents as it begins a new season in their lives. Mother and Daddy lived in Tahlequah when she was born. Laura and Mollie were next. They are Kenny and my girls. Daddy enjoyed Laura's sweet spirit and love for learning. Mollie was next as a namesake for his mother. She is exactly in the middle of the five grandchildren. When Mollie was first learning to walk we were at a wedding in which he officiated. I remember Daddy saying Mollie reminded him of me when I was that age.

Barbara is the mother of the only two boy grandchildren, Paul Russell and Tommy. Paul Russell, Pete's own namesake has the position of being the first male grandchild. Paul learned a lot about working on the farm and knew his Daddy Pete as a cowboy rancher. Tommy was the fifth and final grandchild. He was special because he was the youngest. Tommy was only five years old when Daddy Pete passed away.

We video taped all of us riding horses on the farm when Tommy was about two years old. Those were some of the most fun and relaxed times I believe my dad have. He and Tommy were playing peek-a-boo in the front seat of the farm truck as Daddy Pete rested from saddling the horses. Daddy Pete was fun with the grandkids. They rode with him on the back of a small trail bike. If they went down into a valley or in a bumpy spot, they remember him saying, "Hang on Baby, she's ridin' rough!" He still remembered the Cherokee language he had learned twenty years prior and taught the grandchildren how to sing 'Happy Birthday' in Cherokee.

Pete and Fran treasured their grandchildren, regarding them each special with unique and different personalities. What a heritage the grandchildren were to them. What a heritage and wealth of memories our folks left to them as well.

James, Pete and Earl

The three Simmons brothers had a close bond throughout their lives. They were all very different but still alike in many ways. Pete and Earl were probably the most different. People in Broken Arrow remember Earl as being mild-mannered and quiet. Pete was just the opposite having a loud and boisterous personality.

James was the first to pass, perhaps because of all he went through as a POW in Germany. He died at sixty-seven years old in 1979. James and Arvena had built a house right next door to Mother and Daddy's house. The four of them enjoyed living as neighbors only for a couple of years.

One of the last but funniest times I remember when the three brothers were together, was the Saturday afternoon that they tried to erect a light pole in the back yard between James' and Daddy's yards. As well as I recall, it was Mother and Aunt Arvena who enjoyed laughing at the incident as the three men tried to figure out how to get this light pole, which was quite tall, into the hole Daddy had dug with a post hole digger. The wives acted as though they were "old men" trying to do a young man's work. We took a picture that captured those thousand words. Looking back now, their ages do not seem to be that old.

Pete, James and Earl always had a close bond.

Daddy was most comfortable, especially in his later years, changing his dress clothes into his farm clothes, like jeans when he got home from work. He was a cowboy at heart and enjoyed having cattle and horses for the kids and grandkids. Even when we three children were grown, he continued to take cattle to market and take care of horses on the farm. Barbara was the most faithful to help him feed the livestock and go to market.

A Generation Ago

Daddy liked enjoying the good ol' days and wanted others to experience how it used to be before we had inventions. Tractors are an example of an invention from later in his generation. One time when we were still in junior high and high school, he decided we needed to experience what it would have been like using a plow as in the 'good ol' days' with a horse or mule. At the time we were renting stalls and kept our horses on Judge Righter's farm which was located just south of 111th Street and Elm Place in Broken Arrow. Daddy had bartered some legal work for Dewey Johnson, Geneva Beckham's brother. Dewey gave him a mule in trade. Daddy named the mule 'Dewey' because it reminded him from whom he acquired it. The mule had been born with a broken leg. To keep an animal from suffering, a farmer would usually shoot it and 'put it out its misery.' But no one shot this mule, and his leg just grew crooked.

Our plowing experience was about to begin. Daddy had planted some corn and it was about a foot high. He showed us how the weeds would overtake the corn if we did not plow them out. So he hooked up ol' Dewey to an old-fashioned plow and began to plow. When it was my turn I could hardly keep the plow on the straight and narrow because I was not strong enough to lift it. Barbara was smaller than I, and I am not for sure if Chris was even there to participate. We did not do much plowing that day because poor Dewey stepped on more corn, staggering sideways, than he missed. The corn probably did not survive. Daddy did his best to teach us how things were done when he was young, but the lessons did not always work out. He wanted us to be able to say to our children and grandchildren, 'I plowed with a mule when I was growing up.' How many steps and rows of corn have to be trampled before we can say we plowed? Thus our plowing and farming days came to an end.

Daddy liked to occasionally buy a bag of tobacco and roll his own cigarettes just because it was different. Maybe it reminded him of John Wayne in True Grit. Whatever the reason, he liked to be able to do things that were unique and no one else did. He liked doing things 'the old-fashioned way.' Daddy was especially fun and relaxed with the kids and grandkids when he was down on the farm.

The 3 Simmons boys kept a strong bond through the years: Arvena and James; Pete and Fran; and Mariana and Earl Simmons

Pete and Fran's 50th Anniversary, September 1, 1990.
Left to Right: *Laura, Jan, Pete, Paul Russell, Fran, Mollie,*
Kim, Chris and Barbara

Chapter 23
LEAVING A LEGACY

Nothing Gold Can Stay

One of the things only close friends and family knew about Pete was his love for poetry. He always enjoyed our daughter Laura's visits. His face would brighten and they had the best philosophical discussions. He knew Laura had his same zest for learning.

They had a common bond for the love of poetry.

Laura visited her Daddy Pete at St. Francis Hospital where he spent Christmas Eve, 1994. I'm sure it was not the first time he quoted Robert Frost to her, but on this occasion, "Nothing Gold Can Stay" may have meant something entirely different to both of them. Here is Laura's recollection of their poignant visit:

> *Despite not doing well physically, Daddy Pete's mind still was as sharp as a tack. It was just the two of us in the hospital room, a rare occurrence. I do not remember how we landed on the topic of poetry and specifically Robert Frost's "Nothing Gold Can Stay," but I think it a was divine appointment that I did not realize until after the fact. The exact words we spoke are not as memorable as the connection we made, and I have carried it with me the past 20 years.*
>
> *In my opinion, this four-stanza poem is absolutely beautiful and for those without hope, it's also tragic. If you have never read it, stop right now and do so. Frost was correct, the golden moments of life happen continuously even in an imperfect world. We cannot stop the cycle.*

Ironically, as we sat there discussing the poem, we were living it. Most definitely he had truly experienced life, an exciting, adventurous, golden one. He knew heartache and disappointment, and he felt the exhilaration of rising above circumstances and finding success. I was just embarking on my adult journey and even though I was more "green" than "gold" the reality of our diverging paths was not lost on either of us.

Looking back, I know his early years shaped his life tremendously. He allowed the brokenness of his upbringing to transform him into a defender of the defenseless, poor, and, in some instances, the guilty. Like all humans, my grandfather's innocence from sin was short-lived. He most definitely lived with confidence in his own abilities. The things in life that tarnish also are redeemable.

Tulsa author S.E. Hinton's book The Outsiders, featured the protagonist, Ponyboy quoting Frost's poem and sharing it with others who told him to 'stay gold,' meaning keep your innocence and do not let the circumstances of the world change you. Perhaps Daddy Pete truly resonated with this character because his nickname for my cousin Paul was Ponyboy.

Even though I spent a lot of time with Daddy Pete through the years we had never had a conversation about salvation in Jesus Christ. I knew he believed in God and had a reverence for the Bible, but only God knew his heart. Nothing gold can stay permanently on earth, but with tomorrow comes another sunrise and new life. I wanted to convey that as long as we know Who holds our future, we know life is worth living through the glorious sunrises and sunsets. However, the great defense attorney was not one to be cross-examined. In his own way,

Daddy Pete's words gave me peace that he knew his place in eternity. For all of the things he did in life, this was the most crucial one in my eyes. He told me to 'stay gold,' and I told him the same, and then we shared a smile.

I look forward to reuniting with Daddy Pete in heaven, where everything can 'stay gold' in the light of the majesty of our Creator.

The Simmons, Peterson, Neighbors' Legacy

Charlie and Hazel Peterson, Earl and Mariana Simmons, Oscar Peterson and Earl Simmons, James and Arvena Simmons, Betty Riseling Kellams and Mary Riseling Woodward

I was delighted to pose with John and Bernice Peterson's children and Ellen & Charles Peterson's grandchildren: Jimmy and Betty Lou (Peterson) Stevenson, and Margie and Bob Peterson. We were joined by Verna Stevenson Bebout, Jimmy's sister.

Pearl's daughter, Coralee (German) and Elward 'Cooter' Green and Faye's son, John Edgar Newcomb

The Legacy Continues

Many lives were touched, renewed or changed completely by the work of Pete Simmons. Whether it was in a philosophical discussion with his children or grandchildren, in his Sunday school class, in his law office at different locations, or in the court room, Pete certainly made an impression. Through the years, people continue to tell family members how much he affected their lives.

We had an opportunity to honor his legacy with a 100 Year Celebration of the Life and Career of Paul E. "Pete" Simmons on what would have been his 100th birthday, Thursday, November 13, 2014. The family took advantage of inviting old friends, relatives, former clients and townspeople. It was an especially memorable occasion to hear the stories, whether humorous, serious or poignant. The stories of these special friends were recorded so family can enjoy reliving these memories. Many of the recollections are included in these pages. A wide variety of people attended the reception, aged one to ninety. We believe Paul Emmett Simmons would have been pleased and appreciated all who came to honor and remember him.

Preparing to go home

Mother attempted to make their home as comfortable as she could during Daddy's last months. She had the house remodeled to be accessible for special equipment. When he was released from the hospital, Mother made certain that a hospital-type bed was set up and ready for use in the living room. When friends, family and other visitors came by to see Pete, she made sure the environment would be as inviting and as comfortable as she could make it.

Two days before Daddy passed away, I came to see him. It was

Pete's family celebrated what would have been his 100th birthday
with a reception at the Broken Arrow Historical Museum.
Left to Right: *Gary and JoAnn Smith, Mollie (holding baby Judd),*
Troy and Clay Moses, Jonathan and Laura Hopkins,
Kenny and Jan Collins and Barbara Simmons

a Sunday afternoon, and I had just come from church. Always wanting to be encouraging to him, I began the conversation with these words, "Billy Joe (Daugherty) had a good sermon today. He talked about an evangelist by the name of Raymond T. Richey who came to Tulsa in 1923 and 1924 to hold healing revivals." Up to the very last moment, I had hoped Daddy would want to receive my words of encouragement and healing.

"Had you ever heard of him before?" I continued, thinking I was just making casual conversation. Daddy was weak in physical strength as well as his voice. But he rallied to have a talk with me during that time.

"Yes, I went to that revival when he came to Tulsa. I was saved and filled with the spirit during that church service." Pete would never cease to amaze me. As we both lowered barriers of vulnerability and had no pretenses for the last few years, he would show me glimpses of his life one piece at a time. Much of our closeness began from the time we took our trip to find his birthplace in Oilton. It continued as we went to his cousin's 50th anniversary and another cousin's funeral. And now he was revealing another piece of his life puzzle I was trying to put together.

It was not until several years later that I had a very similar conversation with Uncle Earl about Raymond T. Richey's visit to the Tulsa area. These boys were young, but impacted by that revival service. James, almost twelve, and their younger sister, Kathryn, no doubt had lifetime changes as well. God touched hearts. Seeds were planted. Life happened. Legacies were left.

2004 Simmons Reunion
Left to Right: *Fred and LaVerne Fry, Sandy Walker and Terry Greenwood, Linda Dimon and Freddie Thompkins, Lila and John Collins, Ann and Paul W. Simmons, Earl Simmons, Marian Dick, Jonathan Hopkins, Jan and Kenny Collins, Kim and Jack Hall, Gary Smith, Tommy and Barbara Simmons, JoAnn Smith and Laura Hopkins*

Over 54 years of marriage -- A Three-fold cord is not easily broken.

Chapter 24
GIFTS AND CALLINGS
ARE WITHOUT REPENTANCE

"The Mike Singer Story"

About a month before my mother passed away in 1999, I ran into Mike Singer and his wife at a restaurant. He introduced me to his wife and said to me, "I have a story to tell you about your dad," which was a common phrase I heard wherever I went in the Broken Arrow area. I was prepared to hear another yarn, which typically had a theme of my dad helping to rescue someone from their dilemma. Mike began his story with:

"My daughter Amy was driving through Coweta coming home from visiting her brother who was in college at NSU in Tahlequah," he began. "She was stopped for speeding and got a ticket. So, being a retired fireman, I thought I would be able to help her out and go with her to the Coweta city court.

"Amy and I took the drive to Coweta in hopes of resolving this issue, so it wouldn't affect her driving record. As we entered the office, I approached the clerk's window. I explained our situation and her reply was, 'We don't do things like that here in Coweta.'

"Well, I continued, looking down sheepishly and trying to approach the dilemma with humility. 'Police and firemen understand each others' professions—and I was wondering'....."

"We don't do things like that here," she interrupted.

"Could I please talk to the judge?" I counter-acted, with a mild spurt of confidence.

"No, we don't do that here," repeating her final answer. My heart and countenance dropped, feeling helpless and hopeless. I must have given mental assent to a silent prayer, a typical one of desperation, when I felt a hand on my shoulder.

Slightly jerking as I turned around, I found myself face to face with your dad. 'Hello, Judge Simmons,' I said with a surprised look.

"What are you doing down here? Is there something I can help you with?" Judge Simmons asked.

I gave a quick explanation to describe our problem. He followed the details of the situation intently, nodding as he understood. *"Sure, I understand. Come with me,"* motioning with his hand.

Approaching the clerk's window again, Judge looked directly at her, and said, *"We'd like to see the judge."*

"He's getting ready for a court session," was her curt reply. As if your dad did not even hear her, and before she could think of another word, he turned and entered the city judge's chamber.

As we entered the courtroom, I was feeling mixed emotions: either the weight of the world was lifting, or we have just stepped over our boundaries. Judge Simmons confidently smiled with a knowing of comradery, as he inquired of the city judge, *"May we approach the bench, Judge?"*

"You may," was the reply of the one with the most authority in the room.

The three of us respectfully approached the bench. Judge Simmons' speech was as eloquent and smooth as a well-rehearsed Shakespeare performance. Pete clearly and concisely detailed Amy's immature decisions which caused these repercussions, pleading her case as if he had devoted several weeks of preparation for this moment.

"Judge," Pete proceeded, "This young lady no doubt had a great deal on her mind as she passed through Coweta on the highway. As young people do so often, she was not as observant of the speed limit sign and inadvertently erred in not reducing her speed."

Perhaps the city judge was contemplating his rebuttal, but Pete with quick wit, continued to share Amy's melodramatic dilemma. "Amy has certainly given much thought to the consequences of her actions on that day, and is very remorseful."

Seeing an avenue of intervention, the judge gave an understandable nod and agreed with, "Yes, I see your point, Counselor, I can be lenient on reducing the ticket, but she will need to take a defensive driving course."

"Judge, with all due respect, Amy has college loans to pay, is working her way through college, and this extra added expense to her budget would likely put additional stress on her."

Partially relinquishing, the judge agreed with, "All right, I can dismiss the ticket but it will still be necessary for her to complete the defensive driving classes."

As if continuing to beat a dead horse, Pete brought back his other point, clearing all blame, "Yes, Judge, with all due respect, Amy has admitted that she is in error, but this having been her first and only driving offense, barely has enough time to fit her part-time job into her full load at college, much less taking a defense driving course."

With a single rap of his gavel, the city judge pronounced Amy's final judgment. "Case dismissed."

"I wanted to jump and shout for joy, but as Judge Simmons

gave me an eye of restraint and composure, we concealed our exuberance as we courteously thanked the judge for his mercy and turned around to calmly leave the courtroom.

I felt like embracing Pete in a gigantic bear-hug, as I shook his hand, pumping and pumping it, as if it were a dry well. "Oh, man! Thank you! Thank you! How can I ever thank you enough?"

Mercy and Grace?

But Mike was shaken back to reality as he heard the city judge's voice. The judge asked Pete to please step out of the room briefly so he could visit with the defendant and her father. As soon as Pete left their presence, the judge admonished Amy and Mike, saying, "Young lady, you received mercy in this court today, not because of you. But because of him," pointing toward the door from which Pete exited. The judge continued, "That man has done more for me in my lifetime and helped me more times than you will ever know. I owe a lot to him for his mentorship, the experience he has taught me and the example he has set for me in our profession. So, I remind you, you had better not be caught speeding through Coweta again. You got off lightly this time!" Then he gave a gentle smile.

Both Mike and Amy, though surprised, seriously nodded in agreement, "Yes sir," they replied in unison. "Yes sir," as they humbly left the chambers to join Pete in the outer room.

Because I heard the story twenty years ago I needed to make sure I had all the story correct. When I visited with Mike recently, he added to his story from the first time. He was especially impressed with the demeanor and attitude of Coweta's City Judge. A few weeks before this book was printed, I discovered the Coweta City Judge in Mike's story was Judge Dennis N. Shook. It did not surprise me.

Outside the corridors, Mike began to again show Judge Simmons his deep appreciation. "How much do I owe you, Judge? It's worth every penny of it."

Pete smiled and simply replied, "That's okay, Mike. You don't owe me a thing."

"No, really! I can pay you now or please send me a bill for your services."

"Seriously, Mike. It was my pleasure to represent you," Pete voiced with a satisfaction of having accomplished one more Goliath experience. Then he added, "I'm not practicing much law these days fulltime, so if I can help someone without pay, I feel as if I'm doing this work for the Lord."

Kinder and Gentler

Mike was taken aback. Having known the former judge since he was a young boy, Mr. Simmons had often brought his car in to his dad's station when needing tires or quick car repair. Mike had remembered Daddy being short or curt at times, impatient to get quick service and be on his way. But as the years passed, Mike viewed Pete as appearing a little mellower, or wanting to take time to enjoy a friendlier visit. Daddy's generosity did not seem to be out of character for Pete, but his demeanor was different, as Mike recalled the ticket incident. Pete seemed to be gentler and he appeared to change for the better through the years. Pete always was approachable to young town people, but this time even more so."

Knowing One's Authority

The symbolism in this story is the difference between trying to accomplish things with our own efforts, knowing the limitations of our own abilities and authority, and waiting for the right time and for the right doors to open.

The picture is a person without the proper credentials or authority, coming in off the street and attempting to go straight into the inner courts to talk to the king himself. This is an excellent example of an advocate, one who goes along side to speak for and plead the case for the one who is inadequate or insufficient. Mike's story was in some way like a Sunday School lesson taught many times by my dad.

I Admit I May Have Been Wrong

After thinking about the different gifts and functions in the body of Christ, it was very obvious Daddy had a gift of service. I also came to conclusion Daddy seemed to have the motivational gift of prophecy as referred to in Romans 12. It is very possible to have more than one spiritual gift. One does not need to be a preacher, pastor or evangelist to have this type of gift. A person can often have another profession and still operate in this spiritual gift. Different than the 'office of prophet', a person can use this gift in the marketplace as well as in the pulpit. It takes an especially bold person who is not afraid to speak the truth in correcting others, to help set them on a straight path. A prophet holds people accountable, although it may not a popular stand. They are often loners, and don't have many close friends because of their brashness.

That was something I had never considered before, but made perfect sense. Some men, such as Jonah, argued with God and even ran away from their assignment.

As I reflected back on Daddy's own words as a young boy, I remember he had said he had wanted to be a preacher. But it appears his calling was to take a different path. Because He knows the heart of man, God has a way of speaking to each heart and influencing each toward His Will. God alone knows how to take the hurts and wounds in a child's life and heal them. He alone can complete a person's life in bringing it full circle. I believe it is true in Pete's life that "The steps of a righteous man are ordered of the Lord".

Fran was always a loyal covenant partner to Pete, shown here at Coralee and Elward "Cooter" Green's 50th Anniversary in OKC.

Your Latter Days Will Be Better Than the Former

As if frozen in a moment in time, Pete continued his conversation with Mike and Amy Singer outside the courtroom. As Pete mused for a moment, he finally said, "There is one thing that you can do for me, Mike."

"Certainly. Yes, Sir, ... Anything, Sir. I will do any-

thing to repay you," nodding like a grateful indentured servant, pleading at his moment of freedom.

Pete put a gentle but firm hand on Mike's shoulder, and focused directly into his eyes. With parting but impressionable words, Pete asked in a serious tone, "Do you know Jesus Christ as your personal Savior?" Mike assured him that he did indeed."

Standing reverently and in awe at the restaurant as Mike finished his story, I realized this was the one and most important story about Daddy that had transpired in my life in the last 23 years and as well as an important event in Mike's life. What more can be said than that? No one on this earth will ever truly know how many lives were actually touched, affected and changed by this one special man.

To Be Absent From the Body…

The last time I visited with Daddy, it was only for a brief time. I could hardly bear to see him weak, frail and defenseless. I knew there was not much I could say which had not already been said. I leaned down and whispered in his ear, " 'The eternal God is your refuge, and underneath are the everlasting arms'… Goodbye, Daddy. I will see you again in eternity. Remember, "To be absent from the body is to present with the Lord."

God Winks

Paul Emmett "Pete" Simmons slipped silently out of his human shell and from this world and into eternity on February 6, 1995 in the early morning before daybreak, at the age of 80 years, 2 months and 24 days.

Rev Charles Puckett officiated Daddy's homegoing service. Not knowing ahead of time, he quoted one of Daddy's favorite scriptures:

'What does the Lord require of thee? Love mercy, Do justice and walk humbly with thy Lord.' - Micah 6:4-6

Reverend Puckett also quoted the one I whispered in Daddy's ear from *Deuteronomy 33:27.* What a confirmation that God really does care! Two important scriptures to hear at a time like this. One of Daddy's favorite hymns, "How Great Thou Art" was sung at his service. Every time I hear it on the radio or television, I cannot help but think God is winking at me and letting me know all is well with his soul.

Pete and Fran, Together Again

Although our folks passed away 4 years apart in 1995 and 1999, they were both 80 years of age. They had been married over 54 years. On earth, nothing gold can stay. Flowers wilt, our earthly shells wear out and perish, and although Eden brought sin into the world, we have a Redeemer who lives and also offers us eternal life. It is a choice.

Yes, Paul Emmett "Pete" Simmons, 'your latter days will be better than the former'...

'WELL DONE, THOU GOOD AND FAITHFUL SERVANT; THOU HAST BEEN FAITHFUL.... ENTER THOU INTO THE JOY OF THY LORD.'

Pete and Fran - Together again!

REFERENCES

1900 Federal Census Reports, Creek County, Oklahoma

Albert Publications: *Remember Me. License to Reprint song(1205800) – L150324-9002* P.O. Box 10003, Van Nuys, CA., 1937. Retrieved from http://www.alfred.com

Barr Smith, Robert: *Outlaw Tales of Oklahoma, True Stories of the Sooner State's Most Infamous Crooks, Culprits, and Cutthroats.* A Two Dot Book by Morris Book Publishing, LLC, Guilford, CT., 2008.

Boyington, Gregory: *Baa Baa, Black Sheep.* Wilson Press, Seneca Falls, NY. 1958.

Broken Arrow Historical Museum, Broken Arrow, OK.

Broken Arrow Ledger, Broken Arrow, OK.

Bryan, William Jennings: Retrieved from http://www.pbs.org/ wgbh/amex/monkeytrial/peopleevents/p_bryan.html

Coweta American, Coweta, OK.

Dalton, Emmett: *Beyond the Law,* Pelican Publishing Co., Gretna, LA., 1918.

Drumright Historical Museum, Drumright, OK.

Faith Assembly, 13th and Trenton, Tulsa, OK: Retrieved from http://www.tulsafaith.com/#/what-to-expect/history

Foster High School, OKC: Retrieved from http://newsok.com/

foster-high-school-classmates-reunited/article/2197392

Frost, Robert. Retrieved from http://www.online-literature. com/frost/748/

Frost, Robert. Retrieved from http://www.bartleby.com/119/1. html

Hanlon, Patricia: Correspondent *Tulsa World,* Tulsa, OK.

Harding, President Warren G.: Retrieved from http://www.history.com/news/the-unexpected-death-of-president-harding-90-years-ago

Kansas Marriage Records, 1860-1865.

Mustering Rolls, Kansas Militia, 1864.

Newsom, D. Earl: *Drumright! The Glory Days of a Boom Town,* Evans Publications, Inc., Perkins, OK, 1985.

Newsom, D. Earl: *Drumright II (And Shamrock, Pemeta, Oilton, and Olive) A Thousand Memories,* Evans Publications, Inc., Perkins, OK, 1987.

Newspaper Archives: Retrieved from http://newspaperarchive. com/ ?gclid=CPnX4aOrj8QCFdgUgQodR5gAsg

Oilton (Oklahoma) Gusher, 4 June 1925. "Oilton," Vertical File, Research Division, Oklahoma Historical Society, Oklahoma City. *Profiles of America,* Vol. 2 (2d ed.; Millerton, N.Y.: Grey House Publishing, 2003).

Oilton, Oklahoma: Retrieved from http://en.wikipedia.org/ wiki/Oilton,_Oklahoma

Oklahoma History: Retrieved from http://www.okhistory.org/ kids/lrexhibit

Oklahoma Land Run: Retrieved from www.history.com/this-day-in.../the-oklahoma-land-rush-begins *digital.library.ok-state.edu/.../v004p...*

Oklahoma Ranching: Retrieved from http://www.okhistory.org /shpo/contexts/Region6Ranching.pdf

Prisoners of War at Stalag IV: Retrieved from http://www.b24. net/pow/stalag4.htm

Sherrod, Robert: *History of Marine Corps, Aviation in World War II,* Combat Forces Press, Washington, D.C., 1952.

Shirley, Glenn: *West of Hell's Fringe,* University of Oklahoma Press, Norman, OK. 1978.

Stapleton, Steven L., J.D.: *History of Broken Arrow First Hundred Years,* Donning Company Publishers, Virginia Beach, VA, 2002.

Tahlequah Daily Press, Tahlequah, OK.

Timeline of Radio: Retrieved from http://en.wikipedia.org/ wiki/Timeline_of_radio

Tulsa Coliseum: Retrieved from http://en.wikipedia.org/wiki/
Tulsa_Coliseum

Tulsa Tribune, Tulsa, OK.

Tulsa World, Tulsa, OK.

USS Henry T. Allen: Retrieved from http://en.wikipedia.org/
wiki/USS_Henry_T._Allen_(APA-15)

Wagoner Tribune, Wagoner, OK.

Wagoner Record-Democrat, Wagoner, OK.

Wise, Donald A., *Tracking Through Broken Arrow, OK,* Broken
Arrow, OK. re Tvkv'cke Press, 1987

Check out these other Great Books from
BOLD TRUTH PUBLISHING

by Steve Young
• SIX FEET DEEP
Burying Your Past with Forgiveness

-----

by Jerry W. Hollenbeck
• The KINGDOM of GOD
An Agrarian Society
*Featuring The Kingdom Realities, Bible Study Course,
Research and Development Classes*

-----

by Ed Marr
• C. H. P.
Coffee Has Priority
The Memoirs of a California Highway Patrol - Badge 9045

----

by Mary Ann England
• Women in Ministry
*From her Teachings at the FCF Bible School - Tulsa, Oklahoma
(Foreword by Pat Harrison)*

------

by Aaron Jones
• In the SECRET PLACE of THE MOST HIGH
God's Word for Supernatural Healing, Deliverance and Protection

----

See more Books and all of our products at
www.BoldTruthPublishing.com

Introducing

2 ANOINTED Children's Books

by Missionary Pastor & Author

Daryl P Holloman

2 make-believe characters, 1 ETERNAL TRUTH
You've never heard The Gospel Story told like this!
For children ages 4 - 94

"I used it in my class of 4 and 5 year olds. Great book, the children loved it!"
- Anita L. Jones, Teacher
Tulsa, Oklahoma

Available at select Bookstores and
www.boldtruthpublishing.com

22103103R00176

Made in the USA
San Bernardino, CA
20 June 2015